College Apps:
Selecting, Applying to, and Paying for the Right College for You

Trish Portnoy, CPA, MS Ed

Course Technology PTR

A part of Cengage Learning

COURSE TECHNOLOGY
CENGAGE Learning

Australia • Brazil • Japan • Korea • Mexico • Singapore • Spain • United Kingdom • United States

COURSE TECHNOLOGY
CENGAGE Learning

College Apps: Selecting, Applying to, and Paying for the Right College for You
Trish Portnoy, CPA, MS Ed

Publisher and General Manager, Course Technology PTR:
Stacy L. Hiquet

Associate Director of Marketing:
Sarah Panella

Manager of Editorial Services:
Heather Talbot

Senior Marketing Manager:
Mark Hughes

Senior Acquisitions Editor:
Mitzi Koontz

Project and Copy Editor:
Cathleen D. Small

Interior Layout:
Shawn Morningstar

Cover Designer:
Luke Fletcher

Indexer:
Kelly Talbot Editing Services

Proofreader:
Kelly Talbot Editing Services

For product information and technology assistance, contact us at
Cengage Learning Customer & Sales Support, 1-800-354-9706
For permission to use material from this text or product, submit all requests online at **cengage.com/permissions**
Further permissions questions can be emailed to
permissionrequest@cengage.com

ACCUPLACER, AP, College Board, CSS/Financial Aid PROFILE, SAT, and SAT Subject Tests are trademarks or registered trademarks of the College Board. PSAT/NMSQT is a registered trademark of the College Board and the National Merit Scholarship Corporation. Naviance is a registered trademark of Naviance Inc. The Common Application is a registered trademark of the Association. All other trademarks are the property of their respective owners.

All images © Trish Portnoy unless otherwise noted.

Library of Congress Control Number: 2012948824

ISBN-13: 978-1-285-09829-6

ISBN-10: 1-285-09829-3

Course Technology, a part of Cengage Learning
20 Channel Center Street
Boston, MA 02210
USA

Cengage Learning is a leading provider of customized learning solutions with office locations around the globe, including Singapore, the United Kingdom, Australia, Mexico, Brazil, and Japan. Locate your local office at: **international.cengage.com/region**

Cengage Learning products are represented in Canada by Nelson Education, Ltd. For your lifelong learning solutions, visit **courseptr.com**
Visit our corporate Web site at **cengage.com**

Printed in the United States of America
2 3 4 5 6 7 14 13

This book is dedicated with love and thanks to my parents,
Mike and Janie Sipala, who gave me the freedom to make my own way,
having faith in me and confidence in my abilities—
always right there when needed.

Acknowledgments

I would like to thank my students and Business Education Department colleagues at West Islip High School. To my College Freshman Seminar students and contributors: Thank you for sharing your dreams, career aspirations, and experiences with me. It was a pleasure and an honor to participate in your plans and assist you on your journey.

To my advisory panel of college admissions counselors: Michael, Paula, Manny, Lauren, and Ryan. Thank you for your efforts and words of wisdom. You are always welcome in Room 106.

A shout out to my good friends and support team: Katie and Mikey Sipala, Ellen Fantauzzi, Maria Tavernise, and Tricia Morgigno. Your heartfelt support and encouragement are valued and appreciated.

My professional mentors, Jerilyn Ingold, Joan Rizzo, and Ken Hartill, were instrumental in defining the depth and impact of my work in teaching and assisting students on their paths to success. Thank you for your formative guidance and training during my early years as an educator.

Special thanks to Sue Huscilowitc for her hands-on management style and her confidence in my ability to take college preparation to the next level.

To my editors, Mitzi and Cathleen, thank you for your vision and support in making my efforts to help others a reality.

Arnold and Ruth, my biggest fans: *USPNF—If you study perseveringly, you shall never fail.*

And always, much love and appreciation to my family, Darrin and Jules, for their love and support in all of my endeavors. Thank you, for I am blessed to have you both in my life.

Everything is a possibility for those who believe in themselves.

About the Author

Trish Portnoy, CPA, MS Ed has her roots strongly implanted in both business and educational worlds, but she complements her inspirational, holistic teaching style by practicing meditation, Reiki, and other holistic strategies.

Trish has a professional diploma in educational leadership and administration and more than 15 years of experience in teaching career education and college-preparation coursework to secondary students on Long Island. She has also taught as an adjunct instructor at both local and State University of New York colleges. Enrollment in Trish's college-preparation class has quadrupled over the past six years, leading other school districts to attempt identical programs based on her College Freshman Seminar course.

Trish earned a bachelor's degree in accounting from Lehigh University and a master's degree in education from Dowling College. While holding a valid Certified Public Accounting license, she practiced at firms in Washington DC, New York City, and on Long Island. Trish brings an energy to her teaching that inspires and empowers parents and students to live intentional, creative lives of their design.

Table of Contents

Chapter 9   Online Applications   111

Part V   Costs and Cash

Chapter 10   Tuition and More   131

Chapter 11   Financial Aid   141

Part VI   Theirs and Yours

Chapter 12   Their Decisions   157

Chapter 13   Your Decision   167

Part VII   Success on Campus

Part VIII   How It Plays Out

Introduction

Attention high school seniors and students! This book should be a breeze to read. I've been teaching high school students for more than 15 years, and I know what it takes to keep you engaged while guiding you through this critical and often stressful time.

You have many people to assist you in this process, including your parents, guidance counselor, teachers, siblings, and family friends and relatives. Accept their input and guidance. Listen to their stories, advice, and warnings. Take it all in, contemplate their concerns and guidance, and then synthesize a plan of your own design.

The results of your efforts will be revealed during the spring and summer of your senior year. At that time, you will make sound, confident choices with regard to career direction, college selection, and financial and resource management. Your stress about the transition to college will be reduced because you'll know what is expected, you'll be familiar with the U.S. higher education system, and you'll be aware of its potential pitfalls and risks.

I wish you good luck during this time of planning and dreams. It is very exciting, full of promise, growth, and *action*. Be prepared—you need to complete and manage many responsibilities and requirements. Ask for help and direction when you need it; don't lose focus. From all the craziness, a path will emerge. Follow it.

Warning

All URLs and web addresses were current and correct as of the writing of this book. However, URLs and web links are always changing, so if you find a particular web address doesn't work, just go to the site's main page and hunt around or use the Search feature. You should easily find what you're looking for.

How to Use This Book

It's important to get a bird's-eye/overall view of the entire senior-year process, so read through this book once. You can skim it if you'd like, but there are so many interesting bits and facts that it is important to be familiar with it all. Then, starting at the beginning of your high school senior year, with eagle-eye focus, re-read each chapter, use reference sheets, complete worksheets, and follow checklists in accordance with the timeline in Appendix C.

You will notice the Print This! icon next to worksheets, reference sheets, and various points in the text. Worksheets and reference sheets are available for download on the companion website at www.courseptr.com/downloads. Due to the nature of printouts and online applications, I recommend you use a *three-ring binder* for your college-related materials. You can also purchase dividers to separate your documents into categories, such as assessments, career research, college majors and schools, application and supplemental materials, financial aid, and ultimate decision materials.

To Parents

Parents, you will enjoy this book as well. There is a very clear plan of action for your student to follow, plus opportunities for your input and collaboration. The college selection, application, and ensuing decision-making process is probably the biggest undertaking in project management that your child has ever attempted.

Consider this: According to National Student Clearinghouse Research Center,[1] in 2014 there will be more than 19 million students enrolled in college. During those four years, about one in three students who enroll in either a four-year or a two-year college will probably transfer at some point. Studies also suggest that students on average change their major twice before graduation,[2] and total student loan debt has now exceeded credit card debt in this country.[3] *In this new age of economy, it is most essential for students and parents to be mindful of planning, choices, and outcomes when utilizing limited resources to maximize success and results.*

This text is a resource for parents who have not experienced the world of higher education themselves, those who were limited in their options at the time, and those who don't recall all the steps and requirements that got them there. Use it to familiarize yourself with the process. It is important for you to participate when necessary and support your student.

---

[1] http://chronicle.com/article/A-Third-of-Students-Transfer/130954/

[2] http://www.msnbc.msn.com/id/10154383/ns/business-personal_finance/t/college-freshmen-face-major-dilemma/

[3] http://www.usatoday.com/money/perfi/college/story/2011-10-19/student-loan-debt/50818676/1

The college application process wasn't as bad as I had heard. The stress level for me really was not an issue. Organization is key for getting the components of the process completed. The hardest part was writing my college essay, because it was hard to make it short enough to be acceptable. The best support I got was from Ms. Portnoy, who helped me with the whole process. My parents really were surprised at how much work I did on my own and were helpful with the parts I needed them for. My guidance counselor was very helpful in sending out the applications and information that I needed. Overall, the process wasn't that bad.

—**Sean F., high school senior**

Ultimately, you both need to be in agreement with decisions and plans related to career direction, college selection, personal safety, and financial management. Please be mindful of your student's needs and that he or she deserves the opportunity to grow and succeed in his or her own way. And don't forget that sometimes it takes actual experience more than good advice to get there.

I wish you good luck as well. It can be a trying time for parents on many different levels. Tap into your own network of resources for support and guidance. Breathe.

To School Administrators and Staff

At this point in time, there is a noticeable disconnect in communication styles between parents and teenagers. Additionally, the college application process has changed. College applications are no longer completed with paper and pen; rather, all research, registrations, and applications are completed via Internet-based portals and websites. With such monumental planning and decisions looming, it is even more important than ever to bridge this communication gap while assisting both parties through the career planning and college selection processes.

I've successfully taught career-readiness coursework since 1997, but when the opportunity to teach a college-preparation class arrived, I knew I had found my element. There were no texts or notes, just my own inspirational guidance and prodding, peppered with cautionary tales and current events. I drew from my own personal experiences and those of my peers and former students. I reflected. When I was a high school student, I navigated the college application and career choice processes with little regard to holistic thought and less input from my parents. I relied mostly on an out-of-date tome of rice paper–thin pages, my word processor, and the U.S. Postal Service. I survived, but with many twists and turns and stories to share.

The college-prep course was an instant success. Enrollment doubled and then tripled. Word spread quickly. I was then asked to share this template for success with other school districts, but I found it difficult to duplicate the course without a complete, written blueprint for success.

Ms. Portnoy has been very helpful to me in my application process. Doing the application process outside of school without any help can get extremely hard. It is a great tool to complete them in a timely fashion and correctly. This class allowed me to finish all of my applications on time for early action, and I don't have to stress about them anymore. The hardest part of the whole process, in my opinion, is the essay. The essay itself is easy; the only hard part is finding something interesting to write about.

—Brian G., high school senior

This text is fast-paced, task-oriented, and, most importantly, geared to this generation of young people, the *millennials*. You have the opportunity to offer college-preparation support and coursework using this text either as the framework for independent study or for use in a classroom setting.

Parents and students will sing praises of appreciation for the support and guidance provided to them during this transitional and foundational time.

I can honestly say I would've been unable to complete the stressful, tedious college application process [without Ms. Portnoy's help]. Ms. Portnoy was always available and ready to answer even the most ridiculous questions. The materials available in the classroom—including college essay prompts, books, and other reading materials—and the activities we completed helped me to better understand myself and what I want to do in the future. Each step was outlined for us, and we were required to complete them, which really kept us on top of things. Furthermore, the information on hazing, Greek life, college financing, financial aid, and so much more really helped me realize that getting accepted was just the first step in this process. This was by far the most beneficial class I've ever taken in my four years of high school.

—Kelly D., high school senior

Companion Website Downloads

You may download the companion website files from www.courseptr.com/downloads. Please note that you will be redirected to the Cengage Learning site.

PART I
A Plan of Action

Since my career change from public accounting to high school teacher in 1997, I have had the opportunity to work with thousands of secondary students in their quest for career guidance and college preparation. I see firsthand the pressures that today's teenagers are under—to be popular, to get enough sleep, to work part-time, to get good grades, to be an excellent athlete, to fit in, to perform community service, and finally to get into a good college.

The college selection, application, and admissions process can be overwhelming, causing unnecessary pressure on you and your family. Take a minute and breathe. Step by step, I'll explain the process and requirements to both you (the student) and your parents. Your parents must understand what you need to do so they can support your efforts while not adding any additional stress to your experience. You need to understand the process because it is your destiny in the making.

This is a thought-provoking process. You really need to look deep to determine what matters most to you. What are your interests, abilities, expectations, and goals? I have found that most students care only about the "money factor" when choosing career paths, but through careful consideration and mindful exercises, students and parents can be enlightened to the many pathways to success that abound in this new age of economy. As a certified public accountant who invested $80,000 in a bachelor's degree, only to become disheartened and disillusioned with the day-to-day experience, I now live and honor an integrated, holistic strategy to career and life planning.

Each fall, I am personally inspired by my students' journeys through career planning and college selection. I eagerly anticipate the arrival of spring, when they seek me out to share the news of their final plans and thank me for the inspiration, exercises, and daily prompts that guided them.

Chapter 1
A Journey Begins

Don't be nervous to go to college. It will be the time of your life, and I'm already sensing that I'm going to love my next four years here.

—**Ryan S., Florida Institute of Technology, Florida**

You are experiencing a very important time in your life. The process of selecting and applying to colleges is based on preparation, analysis, and decision-making. It's a major project that you will complete mostly over the first four months of your senior year, but actually you've been working up to it your whole life.

During this process we will take a look at your interests and abilities, your hobbies, the activities you have participated in, and the classes you have taken. These clues will lead you toward the goal of choosing a great college and getting on the path to the career of your dreams.

You will be working cooperatively with your parents (or guardians) and other adults in your life. They can provide valuable information that is necessary to finding your way—regardless of whether you appreciate that. Plan to make this interaction with them as pleasant as possible—both teenagers and adults have a lot on their minds these days and don't always communicate with the love and patience that they should.

This book offers you explanations, exercises, and resources so the college application process doesn't stress you or your parents out to the point that it ruins your senior year. Most importantly, you must set your intention to design a solid plan that will allow you to attend a "good" college that you can afford and that will get you the career you want, so you can live a happy and successful life. That's it!

The college selection and application process takes months to complete; however, it isn't a full-time job. What a relief! At various points, you will need to spend time to complete specific research, tasks, and activities. Don't create drama for you and your family by procrastinating or leaving work until the night before the final deadline. Doing this may also prevent you from completing the requirements with the high-quality results and attention to detail that your applications require.

My first year at college was a great one! I made so many friends and learned a lot about myself and others. Something I think people really have to know is to go to college with an open mind, because there is going to be diversity and different things that will occur, and the best way to do everything is with an open mind.

—**Jessica F., Seton Hall University, New Jersey**

College Application Process

There are more than 3,000 colleges and universities out there for you to choose from. There are probably a hundred colleges and universities that will support you in having a great time, receiving an excellent education, earning a valuable degree, and placing you eagerly on the road to success. As I stated, this is a very important time in your life.

Many people in your life will weigh in with advice, guidance, and pressure. Most people are well meaning, I hope. Some carry the fear and sometimes failure of their own attempts, while others draw from their achievements and success. Consider each through your own critical lens.

For instance, many students have an auntie or parent who *loved* the college he or she attended. They tell "tall tales" of college glory and hijinks, while singing the "fight song" of their beloved alma mater. It is their final wish for you to go to that college. It's all they ever talk about. But, this is *not* the way for you to choose which college to attend. If you would like to please Grandpa by adding his college to the list of schools where you plan to apply, go for it! However, if "Grandpa University" is the *only* school you plan to apply to because he will just die from disappointment if you don't go there, then we're going to have a chat with Grandpa. Our grand philosophy is that it's all about having *options*.

Either way, our plan of action follows.

Questionnaires: Student and Parent

The steps to the college selection and application process are the same for all students. However, because all students have their own abilities, interests, and career goals, there is no set formula that leads them to the same end result. Each student must complete the process for himself or herself to determine the specific, individual outcome.

But before we start discussing tests, applications, majors, or colleges, we need to obtain information about you—a self-assessment. Don't stress if you don't have answers to all of the questions. Sometimes it's more important to know what you *don't* know as it is to know what you *do* know.

Reference Sheet A: Plan of Action

☐ Identify areas of career interest for you to consider.

☐ Understand the framework of college and the educational system.

☐ Identify the major concentration(s) of study that will prepare you for this career.

☐ Identify top colleges that have very strong programs for your major.

☐ Compare your grades and SAT/ACT scores to this list of colleges.

☐ Choose 6 to 10 colleges that include safety-, target-, and reach-caliber schools.

☐ Complete all materials and requirements for applications in a relaxed manner before the deadline.

☐ Identify and apply for scholarships.

☐ Complete and submit financial-aid forms and paperwork in a timely fashion.

☐ Receive multiple acceptance letters so you have *options* when it comes to deciding which college to attend.

☐ Choose the best college for you and your intended major by the universal May 1st deadline.

☐ Consider college life and contemplate potential issues and complexities.

Please complete Worksheet 1: Student Questionnaire so we can establish a starting point for your senior year's plan of action.

Honors, AP, and IB students demonstrate that they really have a real interest in academics. Speaking as an admissions counselor, that weighs heavily in the admissions process.

**—Emmanuel Cruz, Admissions Counselor,
Hartwick College, New York**

What Does It Say?

By completing these questionnaires, we're gaining an understanding of you as a whole person. My philosophy behind career selection and planning is that you should pursue a career that is a natural fit with your personality, with props given to your interests and natural abilities. For example, if you get frustrated when working with others in team settings, then you may be better suited for a career where you produce and manage your own work. Similarly, if you find yourself to be a "chatty cat" in class, then you may be a better fit for working with teams or helping others in the teaching or health-services fields.

Your favorite classes may give you direction into potential programs of study. Are you a math/science brain? A humanities lover? An art or music aficionado? Or a techie? Sometimes teachers can bring a subject to life, but you must realize where *your* interests and strengths lie.

After-school activities are all about options—usually no required courses there. Where are you choosing to spend your time? How can you incorporate this aspect of your life into college and career?

If you need additional assistance in interpreting your results, call upon your guidance counselor. They are underutilized resources, so ask them to read your questionnaires and provide feedback. Actually, go to your team of people who know you and ask them to inspire with you with a plan. Remember our motto: Take it all in, absorb and process, and then synthesize a plan of your own design.

Now that we've had the opportunity to discuss our approach to this project, you are ready for a basic overview of the higher education system, which is the official term for "college."

Making friends is by far the easiest part of the college process.

—Richie O., Siena College, New York

Worksheet 1:
Student Questionnaire

1. To which colleges do you want to apply?

2. Out of those, which college is a realistic first choice?

3. What do you want to study at college?

4. Do you want to live on campus or at home?

5. Which is more of a concern for you—getting into college or paying for it?

6. What are your career goals? Teacher? Doctor? Accountant? Lawyer? Nurse? Engineer? Physicist?

7. To which clubs and organizations do you belong?

8. On which sports/teams do you play?

9. Where do you work after school, on weekends, or during the summer? What do you enjoy about this job?

10. What have been your favorite classes in high school? What do you enjoy about them?

11. Who have been your favorite teachers during high school?

12. Which three teachers are you planning to ask for letters of recommendation?

13. Did you take the SATs or ACTs? What were your scores? Do you plan to take them again? When? How are you preparing this time?

14. What is your overall high school average? 75? 85? 95?

Be prepared: Who better to give insight and feedback on you and your development than your parents? I know you're going to love reading what they have to say about you. It will be interesting for you to see how well they know you and their insights into your plans after they complete Worksheet 2: Parent Questionnaire.

Are you ready to ask one of your parents, guardians, or relatives to answer a few questions about you? Are they in a good mood? Did they have a good day at work? Are they well rested? If so, please ask them nicely to complete the worksheet.

I felt the college application process was stressful. I wish I'd started everything earlier. I only applied early action to one school; I wish I'd applied to others earlier, too. Since I'm the oldest in my family, my parents didn't really know what to do. They tried to help as best they could, but they didn't know what to do, and that made it hard for me. I am very happy I'm done with my applications, and now I'm just waiting to hear back from everywhere. When my brothers have to apply, the one thing I will tell them is to apply early! That is the only thing I wish I did; it would have made the process at lot less stressful.

—Cassidy C., high school senior

Students should be taking a full course-load during their high school senior year. Taking time off from courses only makes the transition to college harder. We don't like to see "senioritis."

—Paula Bachman, Admissions Advisor,
SUNY Plattsburgh, New York

Worksheet 2:
Parent Questionnaire

1. What are your student's strengths, both academically and socially?

2. What do you see as areas that need fine-tuning or improvement, both academically and socially?

3. Which area(s) of interest is your student drawn to?
    - ○ Math/Science
    - ○ Art/Music
    - ○ People/Social
    - ○ Tools/Mechanics
    - ○ Technology/Computers

4. How does your student prefer to collaborate with others?
    - ○ Work alone
    - ○ Work with a team
    - ○ Manage or lead others
    - ○ Work quietly
    - ○ Discuss, debate, and argue

5. How does your student prefer to spend his or her free time?
    - ○ Socializing with friends
    - ○ Working with technology
    - ○ Reading
    - ○ Outdoors
    - ○ Creating or building
    - ○ Performing
    - ○ Helping others

6. When your student was younger, what did he or she want to be when they grew up?

7. Is there a family business or career opportunity that is available to your student? If so, please explain.

8. Has your student expressed a desire to go into a specific career field? If so, which one?

9. What could be the problems or pitfalls that you see with regard to your student achieving this goal?

10. How well is your student prepared for college, academically and motivationally?

11. How well have *you* prepared for your student to attend college, emotionally and financially?

12. Do you have any expectations or restrictions regarding where or when your student can attend college?

Thank you for taking the time to support and reflect on your student. The answers and feedback will provide some much-needed information that will be helpful and directive as he or she transitions into the next phase of life.

Chapter 2
How Does College Work?

Not everyone graduates in four years. So don't freak out when you say you're in the Class of 20-whatever and don't graduate that year. College isn't a race; it's the beginning steps to the rest of your life.

—**Katherine N., Suffolk Community College, New York**

Before you start the application process, you need to understand the framework of college and the higher-education system. Sometimes it is referred to as your *post-secondary education* or *undergraduate studies*, but in this text it's called "going to college."

There are many types of colleges and universities to choose from; they come in a multitude of shapes, sizes, and locations. In this book, I use the terms "college," "school," and "university" interchangeably.

Remember, the ultimate goal of going to college is to earn a degree. The degree is the official designation or document that states you have achieved the educational and practical training requirements in a specific program of study at a school.

College Semesters and Schedules

Each college semester, fall and spring, usually lasts for 15 weeks. Some schools offer accelerated or condensed terms, winter and summer. These optional "sessions" are available for students who want or need to take an extra class or two.

About 30 percent of U.S. colleges choose to split their academic year into three parts. These "trimesters" allow students to have flexibility in course scheduling, elective choices, and study-abroad options.

Whether they are trimesters or semesters, college terms differ significantly from your experience in high school. First of all, there are no full-year classes. Every course runs for the duration of one semester (or trimester), and professors calculate grades at the end of each.

Traditionally, the fall semester begins at the end of August/beginning of September and ends in the beginning/middle of December. The spring semester picks up again toward the end of January and wraps up mid-May. So, if you do a quick analysis, you'll realize that you have four to six weeks off from school in the winter and three months off during the summer months. Did you notice that your summer vacation starts in May? Now you know why you couldn't get a great summer job while still in high school—the college kids beat you to it!

During each college semester you will enroll in five courses, on average. Every course has an assigned credit-hour value which represents the weekly class-time requirement. So, a three-credit *course* meets for a total of three hours per week, divided into two or three *classes*.

Each school may set the schedule for their courses differently. Some schools have courses meet Monday, Wednesday, and Friday for one hour of class each day, for a total of three hours per week. Those same schools may have other classes meet on Tuesday and Thursday for one and a half hours of class time each day, again for three hours per week. No matter which way you slice it, you're still in class for three hours per week for a three-credit class.

Your school may schedule classes using the Monday/Wednesday and Tuesday/Thursday combination, with each class meeting for an hour and a half each day. That way there're no classes scheduled on Friday, which accommodates students who work locally, participate in internships, or want to travel home on weekends.

Point to Ponder

If you plan to go away and dorm at the college of your choice, be wary of a school that schedules no classes on Friday. It may be an indication that most of your fellow students won't be on campus for the weekend. This is not always the case, but it's worth asking the question to find out for sure.

Most physical science and some world language courses require an additional hour of laboratory time each week. You must attend both lecture and lab hours for a total of four hours each week, and you will earn four credits toward your degree.

Sometimes a college offers a course that meets just once a week. If it is a three-credit course, then it still has to meet the requirement of three credit-hours of class time. These classes are usually scheduled at night, perhaps from 6 p.m. to 9 p.m., including a 10-minute break.

According to Table 2.1, you're taking 16 credits this semester. Your Economics course has a weekly seminar requirement in addition to attending lecture classes. Because Economics meets for four hours each week, you earn four credit hours for that course.

Table 2.1 Sample Freshman Class Schedule—16 Credits (Class Duration in Hours)

Monday	Tuesday	Wednesday	Thursday	Friday	Total Credits Per Course
English Comp. (1.0)		English Comp. (1.0)		English Comp. (1.0)	3
	Calculus (1.5)		Calculus (1.5)		3
Spanish (1.0)		Spanish (1.0)		Spanish (1.0)	3
	Economics (1.5)		Economics (1.5)	Economics Seminar (1.0)	4
History (1.0)		History (1.0)		History (1.0)	3
3 hours	3 hours	3 hours	3 hours	4 hours	16 credit hours

Point to Ponder

Using Table 2.1 for analysis, will you have a lot of free time in college? It appears so. As a high school student, you're in class for about five to six hours a day. Even as a senior with a reduced course load or early release, you're in class for a minimum of four hours of class time every day.

While in college, there is ample time and opportunity for self-discovery. However, it isn't all fun and games. Be prepared: In high school, many of the assignments and requirements are completed during class time. In college, much of the reading and many coursework assignments (such as research papers, projects, and group presentations) are completed independently, with class time used for lecture and discussion.

Tip

Current college students are reporting back that they're assigned 100 pages of required reading each week, sometimes just for one course. A good rule of thumb is to be prepared to study one to two times the number of hours that you are in class each day. So, if you are attending three hours of class, be prepared to devote another three to six hours that day to reading, reviewing, synthesizing, and studying your course materials.

Each semester of college repeats in a similar manner, five or six courses a semester, both fall and spring until you graduate. It sounds repetitive and boring, but every semester is unique. Some are really challenging and stressful, while others are easier and inspirational. It depends on the combination of courses that you take and your ability to manage and complete the required work.

In My Opinion

As an accounting major, I completed at least 10 accounting classes during my four years at college. But I also took geology, religion, theater, psychology, and many Spanish classes. Remember, you grow in many ways during college. Another purpose of higher education is to increase your knowledge and exposure to many different subjects and thereby broaden your horizons.

It will be your responsibility to create your schedule each semester, which includes selecting courses and class times. Ultimately, you'll have to meet the requirements of taking classes in a variety of content areas before you graduate, but don't worry there is a list to follow. During your first semester, you will be assigned an academic advisor, who is a full-time faculty member. You'll meet with your advisor to plan your next semester's schedule (an official signature is required), get approval for current schedule changes, and receive general academic and career guidance.

Note

One of my best semesters at college—the one where I earned my highest GPA—was when all of my classes started after 10 a.m. I knew I wasn't a morning person, but it was so obvious that I was a much better student later on in the day. I wish I had figured this out earlier in my college career; my GPA would have been a lot higher.

I had no idea what I was doing. If it wasn't for what Ms. Portnoy gladly teaches, I most likely would have not gone to college. Her teaching abilities were sometimes intense but well worth it because she once went through this and knew exactly how the process should be done. I saw my counselor a couple times, and I really didn't need help with anything. The one thing I would do differently is take my SAT and ACT earlier and take it over and over until my senior year. I think that more people should be able to learn from Ms. Portnoy because she shows you the dangers of college and how serious college should be taken. She describes the differences between college and high school.

—Lansdale R., high school senior

Associate's Degree

An associate's degree is traditionally earned at a two-year, community, or junior college. This degree and program of study prepares you for many careers, including computer repair, networking, automotive repair, practical nursing, paralegal, bookkeeping, and many more. Each college develops its own programs of study and degree requirements, so ask your guidance counselor for details about your state's local higher education system.

For those pursuing an associate's degree, your two years of full-time coursework will look like Table 2.2.

Table 2.2 Associate's Degree Framework			
Time	**Year**	**Term**	**Semester Hours**
Year 1	Freshman	Fall	15 credits
	Freshman	Spring	16 credits
Year 2	Sophomore	Fall	15 credits
	Sophomore	Spring	17 credits
Total			**63 credits**

According to Table 2.2, approximately how many credits do you need to earn an associate's degree? How long should it take?

Point to Ponder

At one school you need 63 credits to earn an associate's degree, but at another you need 66 credit hours. This difference in credit hours should not factor into your selection of schools. Always choose the best school for your career path. Be aware that you must meet the graduation requirements for the school you are attending. The college's course catalog (online or print version) lists the specific requirements for each program of study or major. Each college has the authority to set course and credit requirements in accordance with the state education department and accrediting organization.

Here's a different scenario. Let's say you decide to work full-time while taking college courses at night. How long will it take to earn your associate's degree now? The answer will vary. It could take from three to infinity years. It totally depends on how many credits you earn and at what pace or in what timeframe you earn them.

> **Point to Ponder**
>
> How many credits do you earn when you fail a course? That's right, none. If you experience personal issues or struggle with the course curriculum and fail to meet the requirements, you will not earn a passing grade for the course. To add injury to the insult of failing, you now have the responsibility of paying for a do-over. That's right: You pay to take same course again (and again if necessary), as many times as necessary to earn a passing grade.

Community Colleges

Two-year institutions of higher education were created as part of a statewide system of community colleges to serve the residents of their counties. These schools are vibrant establishments where students of all ages can begin, continue, end, or restart their educational journey.

For many students, a two-year, local college is the right choice because they want to:

- Improve their grades so they can be accepted at a more competitive four-year college or university.
- Attend a school with the most reasonable cost of attendance/tuition.
- Attend a school close to home, where they want to remain after graduating high school.

> **In My Opinion**
>
> Many students hold negative perceptions about community colleges in their area. I believe most of these opinions are unwarranted. Professors who teach at community college are highly trained experts who also work in their fields. They usually want to teach at local community college as an adjunct professor or instructor to share their knowledge and experiences with others.
>
> Also, most junior colleges have open-enrollment policies, so they accept all students—regardless of scholastic ability, age, or grades earned—as long as they have met the requirements for admittance (usually a high school diploma or General Equivalency Diploma [GED]).

If you are a "traditional" college student, there may be the opportunity for you to enroll in the honors program of a community college. Requirements vary by school, but the benefits may include early registration, smaller class sizes, and special programs for academically talented and motivated students.

Junior and community colleges are commonly referred to as *two-year colleges* because on average, it takes two years of full-time enrollment to earn an associate's degree. Even if you aren't planning to earn an associate's degree as part of your college education, it is still important to understand how these schools operate. Also, you never know when you may need to take advantage of a community college's excellent programs and flexibility at a reasonable cost of attendance/tuition.

> *When I went away to a private college, I had my whole plan figured out. I was recruited as an athlete and had a pretty good scholarship to go with it. During my first season, I tore my ACL [knee] and couldn't play anymore. I am now finishing up at my local community college and earning my associate's degree. Thinking back, if I would have known, I would have just started at my community college and then transferred to a university. I would have saved a lot of money and time.*
>
> —**Eddie H., Nassau Community College, NY**

Majors and Minors

According to MyMajors.com, a *major* is a concentration of courses that give a student a basic knowledge of a field of study. There are more than 1,600 different majors available. Majors are then classified into broader departments or colleges, including engineering and applied sciences, health sciences, business and economics, communications, and arts and sciences.

Students attending junior college do not "declare" a major because the intent of the first two years of college is to complete the required liberal arts coursework. These general education or core courses provide a well-rounded foundation of education, problem-solving, and thinking. Liberal arts requirements may include courses in math, natural sciences, social sciences, American history, western civilization, humanities, the arts, world languages, and communications.

For students attending community college at the starting point of their college education, a potential goal (besides completing the liberal arts coursework) is to be accepted at a great four-year school. The two-year school's transfer office and its staff are designed to help you take this next step. Many students who began their studies at the local junior college go on to earn their bachelor's degrees from very selective and competitive colleges or their state's flagship university.

According to MyMajors.com, a *minor* is a set of courses that are sufficient to establish proficiency in a discipline without the student having to take all of the courses that a major would require. Keep in mind that a minor is not a requirement to earning your degree. It is an additional program of study that may help to qualify or distinguish you when it comes time to enter your career field.

I am super stressed, but I am also currently on the Dean's List and in Honor Society. The hardest thing to deal with in college is balancing studying, homework, work, and an actual social life.

—Chelsea R., CUNY Manhattan Community College, New York City

Bachelor's Degree

Careers such as teacher, accountant, financial planner, marketing executive, registered nurse, biologist, stockbroker, and so on require a college education that traditionally takes four years to complete and that leads to a bachelor's or baccalaureate degree.

You have already mastered the framework and calculations behind the requirements to earn an associate's degree, so let's see how you do with this one.

Again, the average semester course load is the same. However, I have known some high achievers to register for six or seven classes, allowing them to successfully earn 18 to 21 credits in one semester. I don't recommend it during your freshman year. Please consider this first year as an opportunity to acclimate to a new setting and scholastic responsibilities. It doesn't matter whether you're attending college far from home or around the block; it's a different environment, filled with many new and exciting circumstances to experience, contend with, and master.

Table 2.3 Bachelor's Degree Framework			
Time	**Year**	**Term**	**Semester Hours**
Year 1	Freshman	Fall	15 credits
	Freshman	Spring	16 credits
Year 2	Sophomore	Fall	15 credits
	Sophomore	Spring	17 credits
Year 3	Junior	Fall	15 credits
	Junior	Spring	16 credits
Year 4	Senior	Fall	15 credits
	Senior	Spring	17 credits
Total			**126 credits**

If you plan your course schedule according to Table 2.3, it's easy to believe that a college education, resulting in a degree at the bachelor's level, will take four years to complete. In reality, statistics disagree.

According to National Center for Education Statistics, only 57 percent of first-time college students completed a bachelor's degree or its equivalent within six years.[1] Other studies report that it takes the average student 4.7 years to complete his or her college degree.

Here are a few scenarios that show how it may take longer to earn that bachelor's degree.

- Student A had to transfer schools because when she finally decided on a career path during her sophomore year, she realized that the major wasn't offered. When you leave one school to begin another, you hope to take most of your credits with you. Unfortunately, there are course requirements specific to your major along with a cap or maximum number of transfer credits allowed.

- Student B changed majors. When you choose a program of study in college, you must adhere to a very specific list of course requirements that must be completed in order to graduate. This is in addition to the requirement of earning a total of 126 credits. If you change from a science major to a business major, you'll now have to complete an entirely different set of required coursework for that program of study.

- Student C chose a slower pace of learning. Instead of registering for 15 or 16 credits, she chose a steady path of 12 to 13 credits per semester. There are many personal reasons for students to do this. The benefits of "quality versus quantity" and lowered stress are only two.

- Student D hit a bumpy patch. He had difficulty mastering the material when it came to certain subjects. He wasn't diligent in attending class, completing all assignments, or studying for exams. He finally figured it out and is on the right track now.

There are many ways to make up for these setbacks. Many local colleges and universities offer winter and summer sessions, when you can take a class or two at an accelerated pace as a visiting or unmatriculated student. Additionally, some students may earn six to nine credits during a summer-abroad session, combining learning with travel.

> *College work is very difficult in the beginning, but it gets easier as you go along. I used to call my mom borderline crying every day in the beginning of the semester because I just couldn't grasp the fact that I had to sit in the library for 5+ hours reading and writing essays.*
>
> **—Carli C., Quinnipiac University, Connecticut**

---

[1] http://nces.ed.gov/fastfacts/display.asp?id=40

A Little of Both

After considering all the options, many students choose the path of attending a local community college. The most popular reason is to save money on their college education costs. Here is how they do it: Students attend junior college with the purpose of earning their associate's degree, which you now know equals about 65 credit hours of liberal arts coursework. Consider that community colleges have very reasonable tuition and that these students live at home with parents or relatives, which is also very economical.

Point to Ponder

These junior colleges have the authority to award only associate's degrees. There is the possibility of attending these colleges for three, four, six or even eight years, but keep in mind that the only degree you can graduate with is the associate's degree.

During their final semesters, students must begin the selection and application processes to a four-year college where they can earn their bachelor's degree. Once accepted, their coursework from their community college will be reviewed according to their official transcript. At that time, the four-year school will determine how many credits will transfer into their bachelor's degree program. Students will have anywhere between 40 and 60 credits transferred, depending on the school's programs and requirements. Students will then continue their studies toward the bachelor's degree requirements, earning their diploma once fulfilled.

Ultimately, the cost savings add up. Analyze the data in Tables 2.4 and 2.5.

Table 2.4 Tuition-Only Cost Comparison: Bachelor's Degree with Two Years Junior College + Two Years at Private College[2]	
Year 1	5,000
Year 2	5,000
Year 3	28,000
Year 4	28,000
Estimated Total Tuition	**$66,000**

[2] The estimated total costs are based on the average costs of tuition for public two-year schools and private four-year schools. Living and housing expenses are excluded.

Table 2.5 Tuition-Only Cost Comparison: Bachelor's Degree with All Four Years at Private College[3]	
Year 1	28,000
Year 2	28,000
Year 3	28,000
Year 4	28,000
Estimated Total Tuition	$112,000

[3] The estimated total costs are based on the average cost of tuition for private four-year schools. Living and housing expenses are excluded.

What is the potential cost savings achieved by starting off at junior college? For some students, this most financially sound plan of action will enable them to get a college education without additional support or excessive student loans.

Point to Ponder

If you follow this plan, when you graduate with your bachelor's degree, there is no notation on your diploma telling everyone that you attended community college for part of your studies; however, your official transcript will list the coursework that was transferred in from another institution.

Study Abroad

Semesters and summers abroad are optional experiential programs offered by many schools. Most students who opt to participate in a semester or summer abroad do so during their junior year, or a summer session around that same time. There may be additional costs associated with this program.

Travel abroad offers many benefits, including the opportunity to hone your world-language skills. Some students participate in an internship or co-operative experience, while others attend classes at an international university. Either way, it's a wonderful growth experience where students are exposed to the global economy, world languages and cultures.

Colleges manage their own study-abroad program or have an affiliation with one from another school. You can research your opportunities with your academic advisor or study-abroad program coordinator on campus during freshman year.

Always read the textbook when your professor assigns reading—it is so critical for your exams and will improve your grades dramatically!

—**Kerri C., SUNY Geneseo, New York**

Cooperative Experience

Some schools integrate full-time, practical work experiences into their academic programs. A co-op program allows you to prepare for your transition to the workforce while applying the knowledge and skills learned in school, and earning academic credit.

Even if your school does not offer a formal program, you can create your own opportunities for growth and exposure by working in your desired career field during summer vacations and breaks. It is especially important to include these experiences on your resume, as they will help differentiate you from other job candidates.

Graduate School

Some careers, such as doctor, lawyer, dentist, social worker, physical therapist, and so on, require an advanced degree. These advanced degrees are earned in graduate school.

Interesting

When you're attending school for either your associate's or bachelor's degree, you're an *undergraduate* student. So, even though you are just about to graduate high school, that isn't what they're talking about. When you start researching and applying to colleges, just remember that you are a *prospective undergraduate student*!

To enroll in graduate school, you need to have earned a bachelor's or baccalaureate degree. Additionally, there may be other prerequisites, such as achieving a minimum score on an admission test.

Here are some common admission tests required for graduate school:

GRE Revised General Test	www.ets.org/gre	Graduate and business school
GMAT	www.mba.com	Business school
LSAT	www.lsac.org	Law school
MCAT	www.aamc.org	Medical school

Point to Ponder

Don't worry too much about the graduate school process, how to apply, and so on. At this point, what you really need to know is whether you *need* to go to graduate school to enter your chosen career field. Additionally, some careers have specific licensing requirements as mandated by the state's office of education or professions. It is vital to know what is required so you can plan accordingly.

For example, Student D would like to pursue his dream to become an accountant. He wants to hold a Certified Public Accounting license, and he lives in New York. At this point, he knows that he has to major in accounting and that he needs a bachelor's degree. What he does *not* know is that to become a CPA in the state of New York (or Florida), you need to complete an extra 30 credit hours of courses beyond the bachelor's requirements. So, he either has to attend a college that offers that fifth year of accounting curriculum, or he needs to plan to attend graduate school and perhaps earn his master's degree.

Master's degrees are required for some education/teaching, social work, science, and health-services professions. It is important for you to research the requirements of your intended career field. Remember, you may only earn a master's degree after completing your bachelor's degree.

Traditionally, a master's program is another 34 to 38 credit hours, which equals 10 to 12 more courses. Some students choose to attend graduate school full-time, while others attend part-time after entering the workforce. It can take another one to three years (to infinity) to complete a master's degree, depending on the pace.

Doctoral degrees are the highest degrees earned, but I'm not just referring to doctors graduating from medical school. There are many programs of study in which students can pursue a doctorate.

Here is a list of common doctoral degrees:

MD	Doctor of Medicine	DO	Doctor of Osteopathic Medicine
DDS	Doctor of Dental Surgery	OD	Doctor of Optometry
PhD	Doctor of Philosophy	DPT	Doctor of Physical Therapy
EdD	Doctor of Education	DC	Doctor of Chiropractic
JD	Juris Doctor (Law)	D Psy	Doctor of Psychology

Note

Even though those who attend law school receive their Juris Doctor, they are not referred to as doctors. Usually, they will be identified as "Attorney at Law" or "Esquire."

I may have to take an extra semester, due to my dual concentration and minor.

— **Mike H., Boston University, Massachusetts**

As part of the doctoral training, most professions require internships, residencies, and/or fellowships. Hands-on training experiences add more time to the process while adding expertise and exposure to professional responsibilities. Traditionally, students who intend to enter the medical profession will require 8 to 10 years of formal education and experience before entering the field full-time.

Point to Ponder

If your career path leads you to a profession that requires a graduate degree, budget your resources wisely. Your undergraduate college is only the first school where you will pay tuition and sign for student loans.

I'm having a lot of fun, but the workload is kind of intense and a lot more than I expected.

— **Richie O., Siena College, New York**

Again, I don't want you to stress over graduate school just yet. But, be aware if you need to both attend and pay for it. Also, you will be accepted or rejected based on the grades you receive in college, your admission exam, and your extracurricular activities/resume. Sounds familiar…

For Parents

Some students have no idea—I mean, not a *clue*—about what they like to do, what they are good at, or what they should go to college for. That is totally understandable. Think about it: How many careers has your student been exposed to in his or her 17 years on the planet? How many totally rewarding careers are on the horizon that we don't even know about yet? New technological advances, frontiers, and consumer demand have the power to direct this new economy.

We allow our children to explore and grow; however, not at the cost of too much wasted time and resources (money and student-loan debt). As parents, we can give our children insight into some general career directions, which will be important when identifying and creating an initial list of colleges.

Go Forward with a Plan

You should feel confident that an interest in a particular career path or program has given you a roadmap for this journey. Most career fields or titles require you to choose from one or two specific majors while at school.

If a bachelor's degree requires 126 credits, that equals 42 courses that you will take over the four years of attendance. Your major concentration of study accounts for about 10 to 12 of those courses. Another 10 courses will be supporting subjects to your major. The additional courses, known as *liberal arts requirements*, include the "rounding out" of your education—everything from English, to math, history, social sciences, physical sciences, physical education, and world languages.

> *Many have this negative connotation when deciding to go to a community college; however, it has probably been the best education decision I have made. You can be an honors student and not feel ashamed. Believe it or not, Suffolk County Community College is one of the best community colleges in nation. If you study and give an effort, then you can graduate from Suffolk in two years with an associate's degree. When you transfer to a four-year institution, the name on your bachelor's degree is from the four-year school, not Suffolk.*
>
> **—Shaun H., Suffolk County Community College, New York**

PART II
GPS Your Trip

Now that you understand the framework of higher education, it's time to apply what you've learned to achieve your goals. This, of course, means that you need a clear vision of where you want to go in life. It also requires you to know about yourself: your likes, dislikes, interests, and natural aptitudes. Along with this exercise in self-discovery, you'll be navigating the intense process of researching, selecting, and applying to colleges. The descriptions and worksheets in the following chapters will assist you through this course of action.

Chapter 3
Let's Get Ready

High school seniors should be taking the time to challenge themselves academically and prepare themselves for the rigors of college. Senior year is a great time to take AP classes, since most of the information will be relevant by the time they get to college, plus they are reducing their cost and credit loads while still in high school.

— *Emmanuel Cruz, Admissions Counselor, Hartwick College, New York*

Not everyone is lucky enough to know his or her life's dream. Some people think it's a miracle to have the comfort and confidence to already know that you want to be a doctor, an interior decorator, a firefighter, or a veterinarian. But most of us figure it out as we go. We know what we don't like, but we have no idea of the limitless choices that are out there, waiting for us just beyond the horizon. But let me tell you a secret: Some of those people (the ones who have always known) still change their minds—sometimes while they're in college and often even after they graduate. As you learn, see, and experience more, you'll reorganize your priorities and your interests. You will also discover hidden talents and expertise. Expect it and embrace it. Growth and expansion are good.

Assessments

Have you ever taken a personality or career interest test? If not, you should. These tests were carefully constructed by psychologists and have been used professionally to accurately direct new employees in some of the greatest global corporations of our time.

Your guidance counselor will be able to assist you in taking one of these tests, which usually consists of many sometimes repetitive or redundant questions about how you like to spend your day and interact with people and things. One of the most popular tests is the Career Interest Profiler, which helps to identify your interests according to the Holland Code.

The results of the test determine a basic starting point for any career or college applicant. It is vital for you to identify your natural interests and preferences. Even as a teenager, you've already been exposed to people who aren't happy in their jobs, who feel smothered and bored, and are just plain angry or burnt out.

You want to be wealthy and live in a beautiful home and drive a luxury car? I get it. However, there is no quick fix unless you are really, really, really lucky. I mean lottery, mega-jackpot lucky. For the rest of us, a foolproof strategy is to become an expert in your chosen career field. Ultimately, this will require you to immerse yourself in your job—all the way. Point being, if you're going to live, breathe, and eat this career, then you'd better love it and have a natural ability for it.

Many students want to become lawyers because they believe all lawyers are rich, drive Porsches, and live in big houses on a hill. But picture this: Let's say you go to college and law school, and you even pass the Bar Exam. Now you're a lawyer. You call yourself an attorney or even put "Esquire" after your name. Now, every day you go to work, you hate it. You just wanted the title and the money that comes with it. Fast forward: Your clients are losing their lawsuits, and some of them are even going to jail because of you and your efforts. Will anyone pay you to represent them in a court of law or a business matter? Will anyone refer you to their brother-in-law or aunt? Chances are, probably not. With no clients and no referrals, how much money do you think you'll earn practicing law? If you're even practicing at all…

Are there doctors and medical professionals who don't really care about helping or healing their patients? Or teachers who don't have patience when working with others, including the children they teach? Sure there are, but it doesn't have to be you.

In many cases, it doesn't matter which career you choose, the income potential is there for you. When you become an expert in your field, you will command a large sum of money for your services and perhaps the opportunity to own your own business. The shortest route to success is to choose a field, vocation, or career that you love and that agrees with who you are as a person, including your interests, values, and energy. Then the time you spend at work will be a joy, a worthwhile experience. You will look forward to your plans, as well as your achievements, and you will enjoy your days.

> *For the most part, the college application process went pretty well. It was very helpful learning about the Common Application and SUNY application. The hardest part was completing all the supplements, only because there was so much to fill out and it took a long time to do. Setting up accounts on the Common App and other websites got me started and gave me incentive to start doing my applications. Also, having unofficial deadlines pushing me forward was nice. If it weren't for that, I most likely would not be done with my applications right now, and I would be very stressed. Ms. Portnoy helped clear up confusion, create time management, and prevent a lot of stress.*

> **—Alexandra L., high school senior**

Point to Ponder

As a member of this next generation of employees, expect to have numerous jobs and perhaps many careers during your lifetime. A key trait to have right now is *resilience*. Resilience means having the awareness, temperament, and skills to be flexible in changing times. It is more of a "go with the flow" attitude or the confidence that you'll end up where you're supposed to be. No worries.

Scenario: You spent your entire childhood planning to become a teacher. You played teacher as a child, you worked at a camp during the summer and babysat on weekends as a teenager. In college, you studied diligently and earned your degree in education. You fulfilled the requirements for your teaching license—tests, student teaching, workshops, and so on—but unfortunately, through no fault of your own, now there are no jobs in education. For a moment, you are dejected—you won't realize your childhood dream.

So sad, but you are resilient! You accept a job in the human resources department of a large corporation, and you become a superstar. You're a great team player, and you achieve your goals with ease. You are a valued member of the organization, and you are rewarded with raises and promotions. You don't look back.

Rankings don't matter anymore, since each school has its own ranking method and regulations, etc. Most colleges are dropping this as a requirement or factor in the admissions decision.

—**Emmanuel Cruz, Admissions Counselor, Hartwick College, New York**

The process was quite stressful. My parents tried to help, but they didn't really know what to do.

—**Shannon T., high school senior**

For Parents

At this point in time, we agree—you have many, many more years of worldly, business-savvy experience than your young teen. However, the rules have changed. The workplace and economy of our youth are no longer here—you can call it evolution or destruction, but the fact is that it has changed.

Also, the interests, abilities, and general temperament of this generation of young people are vastly different from ours. The saturation of technology alone was enough to break the mold; now add the experience of these kids who saw both of their career-driven parents working full-time. They saw the commitment and endless hours, the toll it took on personal and family time. As a result, this generation has a different work ethic, which includes different values and priorities. It will be okay; they may even be better off. They may actually achieve balance.

How does this relate to college and the ultimate success and happiness of your children? Well, they're going to be just fine. Getting them into a good college in order to prepare them for a career that honors their individual interests and innate abilities is the starting point of a lifelong journey. Realize and accept that they may not stay in that career, or even major, for a lifetime or even a year. The young person's ultimate goal is to improve and master skills through education and training, be resilient, and identify and seize the greatest opportunities, so they have the best chance to grow, prosper, and be successful.

The Process

Here is a checklist of responsibilities for you to successfully complete during your college research, selection, and application process. Some items will be simple and quick, while other may be complex and time consuming.

Read through and study the steps to get an overview of the entire process. The remaining chapters will walk you through these steps while offering background information and a framework for understanding their purpose.

Expect to begin these steps at the latest by September 1st of your senior year and ultimately finish by May 1st, considering that most of the work will be completed by Thanksgiving.

Worksheet 3: Checklist for Students
Steps to Application Success

1. Complete self-assessments and questionnaires.

2. Identify areas of career interest and the required majors or areas of study.

3. Register, prepare for, and take SAT and/or ACT college entrance exams through www.collegeboard.org or www.actstudent.org.

4. Visit colleges, if time and circumstances allow.

5. Identify colleges and universities with strong reputations in your field of study.

6. Visit college fairs, open-house events, and information sessions.

7. Determine your list of colleges using an analysis of admission requirements.

8. Begin applying to colleges by creating applications/accounts through:

    A. Your state university system's website, for example:

        i.   New York's SUNY website: www.suny.edu/student

        ii. Pennsylvania's Penn State website: www.psu.edu

        iii. City of New York's website: www.cuny.edu

    B. Common Application website: www.commonapp.org

    C. Individual school's website

        i.   Ex. Bowling Green State University: www.bgsu.edu

        ii. Alphabetical list of U.S. colleges with links, compiled by University of Texas, at http://www.utexas.edu/world/univ/alpha/

D. Paper application (for athletic recruits and special circumstances only)

E. Immediate Decision Days (at Counseling Office)

    i. Follow counselor's registration instructions.

    ii. Provide paper copies of application, college essay, activity sheet, letters of recommendation, and so on.

9. Discuss college choices with your counselor to ensure that you are applying to schools that are academically appropriate.

10. Review applications with parents. Pay fee.[1] Submit.

11. If utilized, enter status of all applications in Naviance's Family Connection web portal under **Colleges I Am Applying To** and request transcripts.

12. Meet with counselor to discuss applications and complete official transcript request and **application processing forms, if required.**

13. Access or print supplemental or informational application requirements, as necessary.

A. Teacher recommendations (2).

B. Activity sheet/resume.

C. College essay. (Be sure to have your essay proofread before submission.)

D. Supplemental documents/additional short essays.

E. Self-reported transcripts/grades.

F. Athletes: Register with NCAA at www.eligibilitycenter.org if applicable and submit student release forms to your counselor.

G. Other materials, including art portfolios, sports and performance videos, etc.

14. Send official SAT and/or ACT scores to each college through www.sat.collegeboard.org or www.actstudent.org.

15. Complete CSS/Financial Aid PROFILE form at www.collegeboard.org/profile, *only* if colleges require.

16. Submit all required documents for supplemental applications via website, email, or regular mail.

17. Review application materials with parents and counselor. Pay fee. Submit.[2]

18. Apply for local and private scholarships.

19. Verify receipt by colleges of transcript, scores, and other documents by December 15th.

20. Complete the Free Application for Federal Student Aid (FAFSA) at www.fafsa.ed.gov after January 1st.

21. Apply for more local and private scholarships.

22. Visit schools where you have been accepted.

23. Communicate with the financial aid officers at your top schools to identify additional opportunities.

24. Select your school by the May 1st universal deadline and pay your deposit.

---

[1] Some schools, such a New York's SUNY colleges and universities, require applicants to pay the application fee before they provide access to supplemental requirements.

[2] Some application portals, such as The Common Application, require applicants to submit their applications after the applicable fees have been paid.

Stay Organized

Most of the college selection and application process is completed using the Internet. You will be required to create and access many different accounts using secure web portals. It is important for you, and sometimes your parents, to have an organized record of your accounts.

Additionally, it's wise to use one dedicated email account and address for your college-related activities. Consider creating a new one before you begin this process. Please keep it simple and appropriate, such as using your first initial, last name, and favorite number.

Use the following worksheet to keep track of your user Ids, web addresses, and password hints.

For Parents

Don't feel left out; there is a checklist for you, too! Your level of involvement in your student's college application process is totally up to you. Some parents choose to complete 100 percent of the requirements for their student, while others prefer a hands-off approach. I suggest somewhere in between.

When a parent takes over the tasks and completes all of the requirements on behalf of the child, it may cause a disconnect from the process, leaving the student without a vested interest in the end result. To support a successful educational experience, it is vital for the student to have invested time and energy into researching and selecting a school.

On the other hand, parents who take a totally hands-off approach to the college application process may create a sense of isolation or underlying disapproval for the student. Even for parents who have never applied to or attended college or even assisted an older sibling, an active and engaged interest in the process will create an environment of support and concern. The following chapters will explain the framework of the college application process, which will allow you and your student to both approach and complete the requirements together.

Worksheet 4:
Login/Password Organizer

Website	User ID	Password Hint
SAT registration at www.collegeboard.org		
ACT registration at www.actstudent.org		
Family Connection by Naviance		
College Navigator at http://nces.ed.gov/collegenavigator/		
The Common Application at www.commonapp.org		
MyMajors at www.mymajors.com		
Fastweb Scholarship Database at www.fastweb.com		
Free Application for Federal Student Aid at www.fafsa.ed.gov		

Worksheet 5: Checklist for Parents
How to Support Your Student

1. Complete parent questionnaires and provide feedback.

2. Be familiar with the process and items on the Checklist for Students (Worksheet 3).

3. Help to compile and detail your student's extracurricular timeline and records.

4. Be knowledgeable about deadlines and testing commitments.

5. Assist student in paying SAT/ACT exam fees or obtaining waivers.[3]

6. Have high expectations for quality work.

7. Proofread all application materials for accuracy and spelling/grammar.

8. Assist student in paying college application fees or obtaining waivers.[3]

9. Work cooperatively with your student to estimate the total cost of attendance for each year of college.

10. Provide accurate details regarding your planned financial support during college.

11. Communicate clearly the expectations of the college student.

12. Manage and participate in scholarship search efforts.

13. Complete financial aid forms in a timely fashion.

14. Attend guidance counselor meetings, information sessions, and financial aid workshops, when offered.

15. Assist when asked. Provide support and guidance when needed.

16. Enjoy the plans and celebrate the achievements.

17. Support the student in visiting and selecting a college before the May 1st deadline.

18. Be knowledgeable and realistic about student-debt totals.

19. Ask the difficult questions.

---

[3] Fee waivers are available to families with "demonstrated financial need" for SAT and ACT college entrance exams and college application fees. Obtain forms and program requirements from your student's guidance counselor.

It is important to start applying and getting that horrible process over with as soon as possible. I have personally seen many people here get stuck with horrible housing arrangements, such as forced triples (three people in an already tiny, two-person-size room) because they waited until the very last minute to get everything done.

—Richie O., Siena College, New York

College work is not a joke. There is a lot of work you have to do outside of class. You have to pay attention in class, too. The tests can be on stuff learned in class and information you read outside of class. Also, it's important to do your homework—the readings and problems, even if the teacher doesn't check it. I made that mistake first semester by not doing the homework because the teacher didn't check it, and I failed a test because of it.

—Steve C., York College of Pennsylvania

Chapter 4
Your Guidance Counselor and Department

The college application process wasn't as bad as I thought it would be. My parents pushed me to get all of my applications in, and they were there for me with any assistance I needed. My guidance counselor was always there with the answers to any questions I had. Ms. Portnoy was extremely helpful with the process. I wouldn't have gotten my applications completed [without them]. There were so many things that I wouldn't have known without the help.

—Nina R., high school senior

Your guidance counselor is your greatest resource. You have a highly trained, experienced professional at your fingertips whose sole purpose is to help you achieve your dreams. It is important for you to take advantage of this opportunity. There aren't too many times in life where you will have this type of devoted, professional support. In addition, the guidance office itself is filled with reference guides, Internet and software applications, print resources, as well as a staff of seasoned paraprofessionals.

Today, most guidance departments and schools subscribe to Internet-based software programs used for college application management, communication, tracking, and more. One of the most popular programs is Naviance, which is a great tool for students, parents, and counselors. It provides real-time, comparative data based on the fate of previous applicants from your school; supports communication and tracking of college visits and application materials; and fulfills the tracking and reporting requirements for students' acceptances, rejections, and post-graduation plans.

Now is a great time for you to go on a fact-finding mission. Using Worksheet 6: School Services Questionnaire you will discover how your school processes college applications, what support is available to you, and what your roles and responsibilities are in this process.

Worksheet 6: School Services Questionnaire

1. Where is your guidance counseling department located? Is it open before or after school? When?

2. What is your guidance counselor's full name? Phone number? Email address?

3. On average, how many times will you meet with your counselor during the fall of your senior year? Will your parents be invited to attend?

4. What is the official name and address of your school?

5. What is the CEEB (identification) code for your school, which is used on test registrations and applications?

6. Does your school subscribe to Naviance or similar software?

    A. If so, did you complete your first-time registration?

    B. Which email address did you use to register? What is your password reminder?

7. What additional resources does your guidance department offer for college research? Personality assessments? Career quizzes?

8. Does your school provide a packet or guide to the college application process? Do you have one? If not, get one (or two)!

9. How does the guidance department inform you when college admissions officers hold informational meetings at your school (a.k.a. college visits)? How do you sign up to attend?

10. Does your school host a college fair during the school day? If so, when?

11. Does your school host a college fair at night for students and parents? If so, when?

12. Which form, if any, is available to request a letter of recommendation from one or two teachers of your choosing? Get two or three copies if you can!

13. Will your guidance counselor write his or her own letter of recommendation? Based on what information?

14. Who is available to proofread your college essay? Your English teacher? Guidance counselor? Advisor? Parent/guardian?

15. What is the unofficial deadline for having all of your application materials completed? Thanksgiving weekend? December 1st?

16. How do you request an official transcript to be sent to each college?

17. Which forms (attach blank copies) are required for submitting documents to the guidance department office? Brag sheet? Application-processing form? FERPA (privacy) waiver?

18. Who is responsible for sending/mailing supplemental materials to individual colleges, such as letters of recommendation, essays, and activity sheets/resumes?

19. Who is responsible for sending *official* SAT, ACT, and SAT Subject Test scores to each college?

20. Does your school host Immediate Decision Days for local colleges, where you can meet with an admissions representative face to face to receive your decision?

    A. If so, when are they scheduled? How do you sign up for them?

    B. What are the standard requirements for acceptance?

    C. In addition, what is required to prepare for this appointment?

21. Does your school host a financial-aid seminar for parents and students? If so, when?

22. Does your community offer scholarship opportunities to local students? If so, how do you receive notification and applications for these scholarships?

23. How does the guidance department inform students of additional scholarship opportunities? Is there a website? If so, please list the web address here.

24. How will you inform your counselor when you have received an acceptance, waitlist, deferral, or rejection decision?

25. How will you inform your guidance counselor of your final decision? And scholarships received?

I'm sure it was a challenge to get the answers, but each one will be needed and helpful to you and your parents as you go through this process. Do not lose this page!

Naviance

If your school subscribes to Naviance, you can access it from any computer connected to the Internet. Your guidance department will be able to provide the necessary registration code and instructions for your initial visit. You can often find the link to Naviance on your high school's or school district's official website.

As previously mentioned, Naviance is a great tool for students, parents, and counselors. You and your parents can access Naviance through the Family Connection portal. Once logged in, you will arrive at the homepage. From there, you will have the option of visiting various tabs.

Colleges Tab

The Colleges tab contains links related to college research and scholarship opportunities. As you conduct your research by college name or matching criteria, there is the option to add certain colleges to your list, Colleges I'm Thinking About, analyze the admission criteria, GPA, and test scores of previously accepted applicants from your high school. When you're ready, you will move some of these colleges to the Colleges I'm Applying To category.

Naviance offers several tools to identify potential colleges for you to consider. The College Search, College Lookup, and College Match links allow you to find colleges based on name, location, costs, majors offered, and/or other specific criteria, using their extensive database of more than 3,000 colleges.

The College Visits link is also listed on this tab. When you follow the link, you will be shown a listing of colleges that are scheduled to conduct informational sessions at your high school. If you're interested, you can click the Sign Up link to register for the event through your guidance department. On the day of the event, you can expect a small group presentation offered by a college admissions counselor with an opportunity for questions and answers (Q&A) at the end.

Note

The admissions counselor keeps the attendance roster from the information session to track each attendee's interest in the college, which includes information sessions, phone calls, emails, and visits. These indicators of interest are highly considered during your application review.

The College Maps link uses a visual aid to present data about where students from your high school have applied and been accepted. Click on a star to see admission statistics for each college.

The College Resources link provides a listing of additional Internet websites that may be helpful to you throughout this process.

The links located under Scholarships and Money can assist in identifying even more potential scholarship opportunities. Please be mindful of requirements and deadlines.

Careers Tab

The Careers tab contains links related to researching and identifying potential careers suited to you. You have the opportunity to (and you should) complete the Career Interest Profiler and Cluster Finder Type assessments. The results of these tests will be shared with your guidance counselor, which allows for greater personalization and direction during your appointments.

The Career Interest Profiler assessment will give you a determination based on the Holland Code. You will be scored in six areas: Realistic, Investigative, Artistic, Enterprising, Social, and Conventional. The areas correspond to skillsets and day-to-day experiences you enjoy.

> **Hint**
>
> When completing any of these assessments, you must take the money/income factor out of it. While rating the tasks, assume that you'll be paid $100,000 per year for performing each. You want to remove the temptation to say, "I won't make any money doing that." The test attempts to identify what gives you pure satisfaction—hopefully it exists.

The results of the Career Interest Profiler will connect you with a fulfilling day-to-day experience and related careers, but that alone won't lead you to a career. At the conclusion, you have the opportunity to add select career areas to your list, Favorite Careers & Clusters. The Cluster Finder will identify potential broad career areas for you to research further.

The Cluster Finder offers lists of activities, procedures, and events. Consider each one, asking for clarification if necessary. Check the boxes of descriptions that are interesting or appealing to you. There may be some lists where you check many boxes and others where you check only a few or none. Each section relates to a different career area. Don't try to force a pattern; it is what it is. The results will speak to you. Again, you have the opportunity to add select career areas to your list, Favorite Careers & Clusters.

When you look at the results of the Career Interest Profiler together with the Cluster Finder, your parents and your guidance counselor can help you determine your top areas of interest. For example, if you scored high in Conventional on the Career Interest Profiler and your top Career Cluster is Business and Finance, you should actively research careers in the business world. Some potential areas to study may include accounting, finance, management, marketing, international business, economics, business administration, and so on.

Believe it or not, this is an excellent start to identifying which colleges you should be considering. Many schools are incomparably great—think Ivy League—in everything they offer. However, even though we would all benefit from an Ivy League education, for most of us it is not available as an option—and even more important, it's not necessary.

> **Great News**
>
> Thousands of colleges are great in select programs of study. Most schools have certain areas in which they specialize. They can be highly regarded for their pre-med program, their school of education, or even their fine art and music programs. Enough colleges have great reputations and programs that everyone will find an option that suits them in preparing for a career.

About Me Tab

The About Me tab contains links to information about you, provided by your school district, which may include your GPA; PSAT, SAT, and ACT scores; AP tests; and other relevant data.

 Located here are links to two more worthwhile assessments: Learning Style and Personality Type. The Learning Style inventory identifies your preferences for studying and learning. The results will be helpful when it comes time to complete your on-campus housing questionnaire used to assign a compatible roommate. In addition, it is extremely important for you to be aware of your own habits and ideals when preparing for exams and completing assignments.

Naviance's Personality Type test uses the Do What You Are Myers-Briggs Type Indicator instrument. At the conclusion of the assessment, you'll be assigned a four-letter code that represents one of sixteen possible outcomes. You will receive a descriptive report that includes a narrative summary and listing of your strengths and blind spots (a nice word for weaknesses), as well as links to suggested majors and careers deemed compatible to your Personality Type.

The college application process was not too stressful for me; it was more stressful for my parents than it was for me. What made it not as stressful was the aid I received from my teachers—most importantly, Ms. Portnoy and my guidance counselor. With the aid of these two, it was very easy to stay on top of things and stay organized. What was also helpful was the help from my parents in that they would have conversations with my counselor, go to financial-aid meetings, and take me to colleges to give me a feel of the college atmosphere. The hardest part about the college application process, in my opinion, was having to type all of my information into each of the applications. Also, cutting down my college essay was very difficult because I worked so hard to write it, and I was forced to shorten it by about 500 words.

—Joe W., high school senior

Reference Sheet B:
A Quick Guide to Naviance

Log In:

To open a Naviance Welcome page:

1. Open Internet Explorer.

2. Navigate to your school's official website.

3. Locate the link to Naviance's Family Connection.

To activate a Naviance account (a one-time-only setup):

1. Under "Are You New Here?" (on the right), click I Need to Register.

2. Enter your registration code (provided by your guidance counselor).

3. Click Register.

4. Enter all required information. A valid email address is required.

5. Use a six-digit password that you will remember.

6. Click Submit.

To access your Naviance account after registering:

1. Open Internet Explorer and go to the Family Connection Welcome page (see above).

2. Enter your email address.

3. Enter your six-digit password.

4. Click Sign In.

Features:

About Me tab

- **Portfolio.** Summary of your data recorded by Family Connection.
- **Favorite colleges.** List of colleges selected by you.
- **Favorite careers & clusters.** List of career interests selected by you.
- **Personality type.** Do What You Are style assessment to determine your personality type according to Myers-Briggs.
- **Learning style.** Inventory-style assessment to determine your preferred learning style and conditions.
- **Journal.** Place for reflection—a great place to share thoughts with teachers and counselors, if selected.
- **Game plan.** Survey that summarizes your plans after high school.
- **Surveys to take.** List of questionnaires (link located at left margin), such as the Graduation Survey.

Careers tab

- **Explore careers & clusters.** Comprehensive, searchable career database.
- **Career interest profiler.** Personal inventory to determine your career interests using the Holland Code.
- **Cluster finder.** Inventory to determine your general area of career interest.
- **Favorite careers & clusters.** List of career interests selected by you.

Colleges tab

- **Colleges I am thinking about.** List of potential colleges selected by you.
- **Colleges I am applying to.** List of colleges you intend to apply to, selected by you.
- **College search.** Comprehensive criteria-based, searchable database of colleges. You can save colleges by clicking Add to List.
- **Super Match college search.** Comprehensive criteria-based, searchable database of colleges. You can save colleges by clicking Add to List.

- **College lookup.** Tool to find colleges by name and state.
- **College compare.** Tool to compare the attributes of several colleges side by side.
- **College resources.** List of additional Internet resources.
- **College maps.** Visual representation of college admissions data specific to your high school.
- **Upcoming college visits.** Schedule of admission-staff presentations offered at your high school.

Home flag

- **PrepMe.** SAT test-prep program (link located along left margin).

Note: Additional custom features vary with individual high school subscriptions.

Other Resources

For those students who don't have access to Naviance or similar software, your guidance department, the Internet, and your local public library have a multitude of resources to provide you with similar information and guidance. Here is a sample of a few that are available to you.

BigFuture by College Board at www.bigfuture.collegeboard.org offers excellent college planning tools, including searchable databases for majors, schools, and careers and information on financial aid, scholarships, and loans.

Next Stop College by The Princeton Review at www.princetonreview.com/college-education.aspx offers *The Best 377 Colleges, 2013 Edition* in both print and enhanced e-book formats, a "best-fit school search," as well as an array of five-minute quizzes in career, school, major program, and study-abroad subjects.

College Center by Peterson's at www.petersons.com/college-search.aspx offers a College Compatibility Tool, information on the admissions process, and guides to effective campus tours and preparation timelines.

The newest edition of *U.S. News*'s Best Colleges rankings at www.usnews.com/college is available in print and Internet editions, providing statistical profiles, tables, and lists of colleges based various criteria. Also available is a web-based, paid-subscription service, U.S. News College Compass, which provides access to extended school profiles and My Fit (school search) Engine.

Marie and Law's *Find the Perfect College for You* (Supercollege, LLC, 2010) matches colleges to your personality type using the Myers-Briggs Type Indicator instrument. The result of this assessment included in the book is a four-digit code representing one of sixteen possible combinations. Specific schools and careers are recommended based on academics and social and physical environments of 82 schools. The final chapter contains a comprehensive listing of colleges and majors compatible with each of the 16 personality types.

> **Tip**
>
> Don't overwhelm yourself with too many resources and their suggested outcomes. Each may point you in a different or even opposite direction. Look for consistency and patterns and consider each source.

Keep an open mind to everyone, because you may get along really well with someone you may have thought you would've had nothing in common with.

—Courtney F., Hofstra University, New York

There is a college for everyone out there, so it's all about the student. The student is the only one who knows what they want at the end, so empowering them to make those decisions is the key idea in this whole process. The role of the admissions counselor and guidance counselor is to be a "counselor," which by definition means we are here to counsel and support students in their journey.

—Emmanuel Cruz, Admissions Counselor, Hartwick College, New York

My college application process was a great experience. However, it was really stressful to do all my schoolwork and get the applications done by the deadlines. I also loved that my counselor was there to help me out when I was confused about making my college choices.

—Hilary D., high school senior

Chapter 5
Majors and Reputations

Know exactly what you want out of your school. I personally took my time and decided for many specific reasons. The academics, as well as the social and sports life, are a great time. I have no regrets in choosing my school.

—Andrew H., Towson University, Maryland

 By using the resources available from your high school's guidance department, you may now have more specific direction to a potential career path or profession. However, another great resource for determining a specific major or course of study is the MyMajors website at www.mymajors.com. You can use the search box to locate the College Major Quiz or select it from links on the heading. Please be aware that this website—and many others—requires you to create an account or profile to register with personal information, including your email address.

Warning

Any time you enter personal information on a website, you are risking exposure. Some valuable resources referenced in this text are free-on-the-web sites that earn income through advertisements and sales. If you receive unwanted emails or spam, please contact the website administrator or look for an Unsubscribe link at the bottom of the email.

You didn't have this spam issue with Naviance because it is web-based, secure, educational software that is paid for by your school district. They do not earn money through advertisements, so you will not receive any unsolicited email or contact from them.

Be Aware

You may be required to enter your Social Security number when completing college applications and financial-aid forms through official, secure websites. No other websites should be asking for this information. Always protect yourself from stranger danger and identity theft.

You can use the results of the MyMajors College Major Quiz in addition to your personality assessments from Naviance and other sources as support in developing your plan. You should be feeling more and more confident in your direction.

Point to Ponder

Statistically speaking, you will have many different jobs and a couple of different careers during your working life. Consider this: You will begin your professional career any time between the ages of 22 and 29, depending on the education and preparation received, and you'll retire any time between 65 and 75, depending on your job duties, savings, and health. So, expect that you'll have about 40 working years to discover, grow, and pursue many of your talents and abilities. This is just the beginning.

You can visualize your working life as a voyage taken by a cruise ship around the world. When you depart, you have a definite port or destination in mind, but as you travel across the sea, you may meet with clear skies or storm, sun or fog, hardship or success. And as you travel, you may want to make a stopover at a certain port for a length of time for any number of reasons. Or, you may decide to change your final destination due to information or opportunities encountered along the way. In the end, you may or may not ever reach that initial destination, and if you do decide to end your trip, you'll do so because it's your choice.

Consider your college education an investment in yourself, preparing for a great experience. Now, you don't know where you will ultimately finish, but you'll learn and see many things on your trip.

Visualization Exercise: Career Research

Many students have difficulty identifying and relating to career goals when experiencing them as descriptions written on paper. Visualization exercises allow you to tap into your creative thought to determine the answers to questions while your mind is quiet.

You can do this on your own or with a friend, relative, or parent. You don't need to share the answers, but you can—and you may even expand on them through discussion.

Sit in a chair in a relaxing atmosphere with no distractions and ask someone to read this script to you using a calm, soft voice.

Close your eyes and relax. Feel your feet connecting with the ground. Take three very deep, cleansing breaths.

Now, I want you to think of yourself in the future using your mind's eye, which is something like your imagination. Picture yourself at about 25 years old (take three breaths): You have already graduated from college and have been working for a while.

It is morning, and you are getting ready for work. (Take a deep breath.) Take a moment and look at yourself; notice where you live. (Take a deep breath.) See what clothes you are wearing. (Take a deep breath.) When you arrive at work, notice your surroundings and your actions and responsibilities. (Take a deep breath.) Just spend some time watching yourself…as if you're on a hidden camera. Breathe.

Ask yourself the following questions:

- Where are you living? In your parents' house? An apartment? Somewhere else?
- What is your location? In your hometown? A nearby city? Somewhere farther away?
- When getting dressed for work, what are you wearing? A suit? A uniform? Casual clothes? Another type of clothing?
- When arriving at work, where is your workplace? In an office? At a hospital? Outdoors? Are you traveling?
- What is the purpose of your job? Building? Helping others? Designing? Selling? Creating? Organizing? Defending? Counseling? Dealing? Planning? Supervising? Calculating? Performing?
- How do you feel about your career? Excited? Satisfied? Content? Proud? Hopeful? Determined? Competitive?

Although this is not a foolproof way to decide on a major career path, it does delve deeper into your personal thought process. Sometimes, you need to quiet the "brain chatter" and use your mind's eye or imagination to really connect and comprehend what you want out of life.

Book of Majors

The College Board's *Book of Majors* is a powerful resource meant to inspire you with easy-to-read descriptions and guidance on hundreds of the most popular undergraduate majors. This hefty tome, a must-have for every guidance department, provides just the right amount of information to encourage you to peruse general categories of study that may lead you to more specific, related majors.

In addition to reinforcing your knowledge and awareness of popular career fields and their requirements, the College Board's *Book of Majors* offers an unparalleled opportunity to explore professional opportunities that you may not have known existed.

Putting It All Together

By this point, you have already accomplished a lot. Thinking things through and completing preparation exercises makes the process so much more straightforward for you. To solidify your plan, complete Worksheet 7: Putting It All Together to organize your thoughts. You should share your completed responses with your guidance counselor and your parents. They may be able to identify patterns and connections based on their many years of experience.

For me, the college application process was very stressful. Because I have absolutely no idea where I want to go, it makes choosing schools harder. I don't know geographically where I want to be. Sometimes I'll think I want to go to Florida or far away, but then another day I'll feel like I want to stay home.

—Victoria C., high school senior

College fairs are overwhelming but beneficial. I encourage students to gather information from the schools they are considering and then take it home and read it through. At that point, they can separate their college choices by low-, medium-, and high-interest categories.

—Paula Bachman, Admissions Advisor, SUNY Plattsburgh, New York

It was a bit stressful knowing that any mistake could affect the decisions of colleges. I tried to keep organized and do a little at a time so that the work didn't build up. This made it easier to not make mistakes. The hardest part was choosing the colleges that I wanted to apply to. My guidance counselor and Ms. Portnoy helped a lot in getting everything done correctly. My parents supported all of my decisions and added a few colleges to my list to make sure I had a decent number of options. I'm glad it's over now and can't wait for the decisions.

—Caitlin D., high school senior

Worksheet 7:
Putting It All Together

1. Which two careers were you considering before you started this process?

2. What are your two highest scoring categories according to the Career Interest Profiler or another Holland Code Assessment?

3. What are your two top career areas according to the Cluster Finder or another career assessment?

4. Reflecting on your responses, what are the similarities between these six career areas?

5. Reflecting again on your responses, what are the differences in these six career areas?

6. Which two or three career areas hold the most interest and potential for you?

7. What is the job outlook for these careers? Search your career title(s) using either Naviance's Career tab or the Job Outlook link while accessing the *Occupational Outlook Handbook* online at www.bls.gov/ooh for these answers.

8. What is the average salary for these careers? Search your career title(s) using either Naviance's Career tab or the Pay link while accessing the *Occupational Outlook Handbook* online at www.bls.gov/ooh for these answers.

9. To prepare for these career fields, what are the required college majors or programs of study? Search your career title(s) using either Naviance's Career tab or the How to Become One link while accessing the *Occupational Outlook Handbook* online at www.bls.gov/ooh for these answers.

10. Are there licensing or certification requirements for your career fields?

11. Will you need a graduate degree, such as a master's or doctorate degree, to enter these career fields?

12. Are you interested in earning a double major or a minor in any other areas of study?

13. Are internships, co-op programs, field studies, or student-teaching experiences required for entry into your chosen fields?

14. Would you be interested in participating in study-abroad for a semester, summer, or full-year program?

15. If so, where are you interested in traveling to, and what would you like to learn/study/experience while you are there?

Reputations Matter

In case you didn't notice, you just created a career plan that included identifying the major(s) that you intend to study while in college. If you missed it, re-read your answer to Question 9. Your college major(s) provide needed information to start researching and considering colleges for application. According to Reference Sheet A: Our Plan of Action, we now have to create a list of 20 colleges that have highly regarded and recommended reputations for your area(s) of study.

When enrolled in college, you're paying for the opportunity to attend classes, broaden your horizons, hone your analytical mind and problem-solving skills, improve your writing skills, and develop your language and vocabulary. During which you're also expanding your mind with a broad scope of coursework, including independent and group/cooperative learning, speaking, and presenting.

Ultimately, what you are really paying for is the reputation of that particular school's methods and abilities in preparing and training future professionals in their chosen career field.

The entire college selection, application, and decision process comes down to this: When selecting your school, choose the college with the best reputation for your major, where you have been accepted, and that you can pay for without causing too much present or future stress on your financial resources.

Warning

At the age of 18 or 19, it seems quite painless to sign a few papers that require you to pay back money at a certain interest rate sometime in the future (when you are 23). It's like a lifetime away, and there's minimal difference on the loan documents whether you are borrowing $5,000, $15,000, or $50,000. Only when you are 23, working 50 hours a week at your first job, buying new work clothes, upgrading your car, living in your own apartment, and having a social life, remember that these student loans will be waiting patiently for you. They will be a part of your life for at least the next 10 years, waiting to take their share of your disposable income, or "fun money."

College fairs are a great way to get literature on potential colleges and speak with representatives. They are also a great opportunity to be exposed to colleges that you may never have heard of.

—Ryan Neary, Admissions Advisor, SUNY Farmingdale, New York

Admissions counselors will tell you that their college is great for you, your major, or your special interest. It's their job to boost the number of applicants and potential enrollees to their school. Some schools will offer immediate scholarships and grants to students who fit a specific need, including high SAT/ACT scores, high GPA, special talents, or athletics. Make sure the school fits your needs before you consider filling theirs.

Consider this: At your top-choice school, the admissions staff needs to fill all spots available for their freshman class. In a perfect world, these students have an A+ GPA and 1600 on the Math and Critical Reading sections of the SATs. Fortunately for you, me and many other students, not all A+/1600 students want to go to that school, so now the admissions reps have to recruit and eventually admit students with lower GPAs and test scores until all the spots are taken.

It is a question of supply and demand. All schools want to admit the highest-achieving students, but those students have *choices* with regard to which *amazing* school to attend. But basically, you all have choices as to which amazing school you can apply to, be accepted at, and attend.

> **Note**
> Schools want to attract the best students out there, and by doing so they make their school more competitive and more prestigious, which allows an excellent program to speak for itself.

Rankings

The Internet is full of rankings, ratings, and opinions on the best colleges. When judging the content, it is best to understand the methods used and the independence of the system.

Rugg's Recommendations on the Colleges

Rugg's Recommendations on the Colleges, available at your guidance department or for purchase at www.ruggsrecommendations.com, does an excellent job of rating more than 1,100 schools across the nation according to majors and programs. Mr. Rugg has been publishing his independent reference book for the last 20 years, which makes his text a necessity for every counselor and college-preparation professional.

> **Note**
> You and your guidance counselor will determine the mix of schools to which you should apply. The number of Most Selective, Highly Selective, and Selective colleges will be based on your academic record, test scores, intended major, and personal characteristics.

Mr. Rugg's evaluation system ranks schools by three categories: Most Selective, Highly Selective, and Selective. These categories correspond to acceptance rates, average GPA, and admission-test scores at each college. Schools are also identified by the size of student body using broad categories: small, moderate, medium, large, and extra large.

Rugg's process identifies colleges with the best reputation by major program as determined by industry professionals. Who better to gauge the preparation and competencies of a program of study than the industry professionals who ultimately hire graduates from these colleges to work for their firms, companies, and corporations?

Using this text, you can look up your major, such as religious studies, psychology, or business management, to easily identify which schools have the best reputation for that program. Rugg's also includes an alphabetical listing of colleges and the recommended majors/programs. For example, you can look up XYZ University to find that they have excellent programs in math, biology, marine science, and physics. This section, a great indicator of the overall strength of the school and its specific, highly regarded departments, includes average admissions-test scores and detailed contact information.

Check with your counselor or guidance department to determine whether *Rugg's Recommendations on the Colleges* is available for use. Current editions are available in digital format, while past editions are in print.

> **In My Opinion**
>
> A great reason to add a school to your list is when you know it has an excellent reputation in *two* or more areas of study that you are considering. At 17 years old, you don't have the life experience or worldliness to grasp the potential depth and breadth of certain areas of study. In other words, it may take you two or three classes in the subject to really know whether you want to commit to the major.

U.S. News & World Report

At www.usnews.com/college, *U.S. News & World Report* offers comprehensive college rankings both online and in a print edition. Their online services include basic access to their rankings and lists, with paid subscription access to their guides and College Compass portal. *U.S. News*'s listings include ranking of national and regional colleges, best-value schools, historically black colleges, and business, engineering, and teaching schools.

Bloomberg's Businessweek

At www.businessweek.com/bschools/rankings, *Bloomberg Businessweek* compiles their ranking of best undergraduate business schools while devoting part of their website to B-School news and analysis of market and job conditions.

Local Industry Professionals

This is another great resource to tap to discover strong programs and colleges. Contact your local professional organization; they usually have an education outreach committee that can assist you and provide you with suggestions.

If you want to pursue a career in nursing, but you don't know which colleges have strong programs and reputations, contact the Human Resources department at a few highly regarded hospitals and medical offices to ask them for a list of colleges where they recruit new hires. You will see a pattern emerge when the same colleges appear on different organizations' lists. You can use this same method in any career field, including business professionals, teachers, engineers, computer programmers, artists, dancers, bankers, stockbrokers, veterinarians, and journalists.

Declaring Your Major

In most schools, you have to declare a major by the first semester of your junior/third year of school. The declaration process is quite simple: All you need to do is complete a form, have your advisor sign it, and submit it to the registrar's office.

Right now it appears as if you have plenty of time to make a decision; however, it may cost you. For instance, let's say you're pursuing a business administration major. For the first two years of college, you follow the list of recommended courses while adding your choice of electives. You're a student in good standing in the College of Business and Economics at your university. During the summer before junior year, you decide to switch and declare your major in occupational therapy (OT).

You chose this major because your cousin is being treated by an occupational therapist, and his progress is transformational. Also, you vaguely remember that you were a great student in your health and science classes in high school, but you never thought about OT as a major.

So, you think you're in good shape because you didn't begin your junior-year coursework yet. But when you meet with your advisor, you learn that you have to do an internal transfer (official paperwork) to be accepted to the College of Health Sciences, and that all the business and economics classes you took only count as electives. Because you now need to take the required biology, chemistry, and health-science courses, you just delayed your graduation date by a full year, if not two, which means more money for tuition and possibly room and board.

Point to Ponder

Yes, it is true that you can declare your major as far in as your third year of college, but remember that in actuality you are preparing for a specific major the moment you step on campus for your freshman year.

I was lucky enough to complete my college application process through my coach because of sports. As I am only applying to one school, many people think I have it easy. Just because before school started I knew where I was going to play lacrosse, teachers and students gave me trouble, like, "Oh sorry...I'm not like you and already know where I'm going." Little did they know that I had to do the same thing that they are doing now, but I started earlier and had it harder. Instead of just applying to colleges, I had to apply, meet coaches, meet teammates, stress over scholarship money and playing time when I get to college, and see which team would accept me the best. Now that my application is complete and my papers are signed, I am excited to attend.

—**Kyle C., high school senior**

List of Schools

It is now time to compile your initial list of 20 to 30 colleges that have excellent programs for your specific major. It may seem like too many, but soon you will consider other important factors that will help you to trim your list down to the 6 to 10 schools to which you will apply.

> **Tip**
>
> The National Association for College Admissions Counseling (NACAC) at www.nacacnet.org provides many great resources for students and their parents to assist in navigating the college application and financial-aid processes. This organization also sponsors NACAC National College Fairs held around the country. For a schedule of fall events, visit their website at www.nacacnet.org/college-fairs/FallNCF/Pages/default.aspx. You should know in advance that even though there may not be an admission fee, you may be charged a parking fee. Attend this popular, often crowded event to research potential schools, pick up informational brochures, network with admissions representatives, and actively express your interest in participating colleges of your choice.

When adding a school to your list, determine its category: Highly Selective, Selective, or Moderately Selective. If you're referencing Rugg's text, he does it for you. If not, use the school's admissions data, such as the percentage of admitted applicants or the average SAT or ACT scores for last year's admitted students.

Table 5.1 will help you categorize your schools. You'll find required information on The College Board's BigFuture website at www.bigfuture.collegeboard.org, under the Applying link, or on each college's official website by using the link or searching for "Admission Quick Facts."

Category	Average SAT Range (Critical Reading and Math sections only)	Average ACT Range (Composite)	Percent of Applicants Admitted
Highly selective	1300–1600	27–36	15% or less
Selective	1100–1300	24–26	15%–35%
Moderately selective	950–1100	21–24	35%–50%

Table 5.1 School Categorization

Rugg's Recommendations on the Colleges also references the size of each school by code, according to the number of students. Or you can use The College Board's BigFuture website at www.bigfuture.collegeboard.org, under the link Campus Life, or each college's official website by using the link or searching for "Admission Quick Facts."

Use Worksheet 8: Initial List of Schools to record the results of your research. If you are considering two or more potential majors, use a separate worksheet for each program of study.

> *I thought the college application process was stressful, but it was relatively easy. I was able to be more open to away colleges, and I realized that there are a lot of colleges out there. The process was overwhelming at first because I had to backtrack literally every aspect of my life the past 17 years. I do feel that Ms. Portnoy helped me get motivated to get things done and to really understand that I could do the applications on my own, and it was me who did it.*
>
> **—Katrina L., high school senior**

> *My professors are all right, but I much prefer high school teachers. I have two big lecture halls, one of which I fell asleep in today and the other of which is pretty interesting. The classes are a lot less personal with the teacher-student relationship, but that is pretty much a given.*
>
> **—Joe S., Penn State University, Pennsylvania**

> *I am currently taking 18 credits and studying to be a mechanical engineer. My courses are calculus, microeconomics, chemistry, university experience, and intro to mechanical engineering. The only thing I can say about schedule is to have good time management. My days are mostly spent in class or studying.*
>
> **—Ryan S., Florida Institute of Technology, Florida**

Worksheet 8:
Initial List of Schools

Intended Major:

School Name, State	Category (Most Selective, Highly Selective, Selective)	Size (Small, Moderate, Medium, Large, Extra Large)

PART III
Components of the College Application

There are many elements of a college application, all of which are considered when determining your college admissions decision. Some parts count more than others, including evaluation of your high school transcript and college entrance exam test scores. Most colleges require additional materials to be submitted, called the Supplemental Application, which includes college essay(s), extracurricular activity record, and letters of recommendation.

Many students consider the college application process stressful because they haven't yet had to manage or complete a project as large and important as this one. You need to stay organized; create, complete, and compile required documents; and meet or beat deadlines.

Chapter 6
The Big Three: Academic Index

We look at the rigor of the high school curriculum. We always like to see a student challenging themselves by taking advanced courses whenever possible. However, we only encourage a student to take advanced courses if they can be successful. We would rather see a student take a regular math course and get an A than an accelerated math class and get a C.

—Paula Bachman, Admissions Advisor, SUNY Plattsburgh, New York

The top three factors in determining whether a student gets accepted to or rejected from a college are course selection and rigor, grade-point average, and college admission test scores. These factors make up the applicant's *academic index*, which is the primary method of categorizing applicants.

Extracurricular activities, including sports and clubs, honors and awards, letters of recommendation, and college essays, provide insight into the energy, effort, interest, and dedication of the student. These are supporting factors in determining admission, especially when comparing two applicants with similar academic indexes.

Course Selection and Vigor

Your academic record begins in ninth grade, or even earlier if you completed accelerated math or language courses. On that very day, did you and your parents know about what really matters when getting into college? Hopefully, you were told that the college application process doesn't begin in the fall of senior year; it began on the day you made your course schedule.

There are various opportunities to take accelerated, honors, college-level, advanced placement, and International Baccalaureate coursework in high school. Most of those recommendations are made by your teachers and guidance counselor, based on your achievement and grades in certain subjects. If you are successful and excel in your courses, be prepared to push yourself to study advanced or high-level content.

In addition, competitive colleges expect four years of physical science and math on their applicant's transcript. **Do not stop taking these courses just because you met the requirements to graduate high school. There is much more learning ahead.**

College admissions committees are looking to admit students who successfully challenge themselves. Let me emphasize the word "successfully." When a student is enrolled in any higher-level course, it is expected that the student will commit and obtain mastery of the subject. It is in no one's best interest to see an honors-level course with a final grade of C or below.

Senior year is when most students expect to sit back and relax after a stressful junior year, but that is not the case. College admissions officers are looking specifically at your senior-year course load as a means to judge your level of commitment to learning and education.

Point to Ponder

Many high school seniors take advantage of "early release" programs if they're available. This opportunity allows students to take only the minimum required course load for graduation while maintaining full-time status. This reduced schedule has you missing the opportunity to further enhance or expand your studies with two or maybe three additional classes. The surprising thing is that many students choosing early release go home to rest, only to have to return to high school an hour or two later to participate in sports, the arts, clubs, and/or other afterschool activities.

If your high school offers electives in diverse areas of study, take advantage of them. Use them to further identify what you're good at and what you enjoy. Each elective area supports a potential career path or major.

As a warning, keep in mind that students who use their senior year to detach from the vigor and high expectations of school and education are creating an uphill climb once they reach college.

Another potential area of disconnect between high school and college is in the amount of independent reading required to successfully prepare for class. In high school, most reading assignments, except in English literature courses, are not necessary, allowing most students to be successful by attending class and taking notes, but not reading the text.

Cautionary Tale

Students who choose not to take math during their senior year may often feel as if they've hit the jackpot. However, when these same students get to college, they are required to complete at least two college-level math courses, no matter which major they've chosen. Remember, a college education requires you to be well-rounded and educated in many disciplines.

Consider this: College-level math is calculus, not algebra, geometry, or trigonometry. After taking a full year off of math studies and practice, you will be expected to pass Calculus I and II.

In college it's a whole different ballgame. Each college professor will have his or her own style of teaching and preparation. Some professors will outline the chapter in their notes and prepare the exam based on these notes. Other professors will use class time to discuss anecdotal stories related to (or not related to) the chapter material and will base the exam on the assigned reading. Be prepared!

Grade-Point Average and Rank

Every high school calculates grade-point average (GPA) differently, according to their preferred methodology. Some high schools use a 100-point scale, and others use letter grades (A, B, C) and calculate GPA based on a 4.0 or 5.0 scale. GPA is the calculation of the average of all the courses you've completed. Your official high school transcript reflects your GPA calculated using your final grades in the courses completed by the end of your junior year.

Each high school can calculate GPA according to its own formula, some include physical education grades in the calculation, while others do not. Some high schools include grades from elective coursework, while others include only the five major academic subjects. And again, some high schools choose to assign more importance to classes that carry honors, AP, college-level, or IB distinction. This allows for a weighted GPA where students can achieve a 104.4 on a 100-point scale or 4.3 on a 4.0 scale.

Due to the differences in calculating and reporting GPA across the country, college admissions officers recalculate your GPA based on their own methods in order to compare you fairly to other students, or apples to apples.

Rank is the numerical order of graduating students from your high school, based on GPA from highest to lowest. It's difficult to compare ranking across high schools considering different grading criteria, course offerings, and levels, so most admissions staff don't use this as a component to the application. Accordingly, more and more high schools are not even calculating and publicizing the rank of their graduates.

Self-reporting grades is a new trend where colleges are allowing (or even requiring) students to submit their grades. This requires you to access a secure website to enter each course and grade as it appears on your transcript. Ultimately, this allows the admissions department to have access to your academic history without waiting to receive a copy of your transcript. Even more importantly, when you enter each course, level, and grade separately, admission officers can categorize and recalculate your GPA easily at their discretion.

Colleges base their admission decisions on these self-reported grades. When you choose to attend and commit to a particular school, the admissions department will expect a final, official transcript from your guidance department after you graduate. Upon receipt, the admissions staff will compare, line by line, each course and grade. If there are major discrepancies between the self-reported and official transcripts, the university has the right to revoke your acceptance.

College Admissions Tests

Most colleges require you to submit scores from either the SAT (Scholastic Aptitude Test) or the ACT (formerly known as the American College Test) admission exam. Traditionally, you take the either one or both of these exams in spring of your junior year, which allows you the opportunity to retake one or more tests in the fall as a senior, if necessary.

A growing number of colleges don't include college admission test scores as a required element in the application process. If you apply to any of these schools, then you have one less thing to do for those applications, but most likely you will still need to take either one of the tests for the other colleges on your list. The National Center for Fair and Open Testing maintains a listing of test-optional schools at www.fairtest.org.

> **Point to Ponder**
>
> There is much debate over the value of judging students' college readiness, aptitude, and future success through admission tests. Either way, if even one college will use your scores to determine your admittance, then you'd better prepare well for the exam.

SAT versus ACT: What Is the Difference?

Most schools accept either SAT or ACT scores to satisfy their college admission test requirement. Each has a different scoring scale, number of sections, subject matter covered, and duration.

The one definite is that you need to *prepare* for these tests over a period of time, not just the night or weekend before. These tests aren't designed for you to show up cold, as they do not measure intelligence (IQ). Rather, they're used to predict your success in college while comparing you globally to all other applicants using standardized testing.

Check with your guidance counselor regarding the availability of resources, courses, tutors, and support services to prepare for these important exams. There are crucial test-taking strategies that may go against what you learned in high school. Some include when to guess and when to omit an answer, as well as which questions to skip altogether, given that the time required to correctly answer the question may prevent you from completing the remaining questions.

> **Current Events**
>
> Recent test scandals have rocked the college admissions world. Increased security measures, both at registration and at test centers, have been instituted to ensure the correct identity of test-takers. Maintaining the validity of college admission test scores provides fairness to all applicants, so be patient with the process.

Should You Take the SAT or ACT?

The answer to this question really depends on your strengths and weaknesses as a student; on using your brain and memory; on your problem-solving skills, time management, and knowledge of vocabulary; and on your level of mastery of mathematics, etc.

Realistically, you can take either test. Most colleges and universities accept them interchangeably in the admissions process.

The schedule and comparison of tests is as follows:

SAT	Testing Dates	ACT	Testing Dates
• Scored on a 200- to 800-point scale for each content area (2400 highest combined score) • ¼ point off for incorrect answers **Content areas include:** • Math (3 sections) • Critical Reading (3 sections) • Writing (3 sections) • Field Test/ Experimental (1 section) • 10 sections in total • Includes Geometry and Algebra II • Measures critical thinking and analytical reasoning Register at www.collegeboard.org	January March/April **May** June October **November** December	• Scored on a 1- to 36-point scale (averaged for a composite score) • No penalty for incorrect answers **Content areas include:** • English • Math • Reading • Science Reasoning • 4 sections in total • Optional ACT plus Writing Section • Includes Trigonometry and Grammar • Curriculum-based questions Register at www.actstudent.org	February April **June** September **October** December

Accommodations are available to students with disabilities and those who have religious objections to Saturday testing. Fee waivers are available to students who demonstrate financial need. Your guidance counselor can assist you with these arrangements, if applicable.

In order to calculate the GPA for admissions, we do not include any courses that are not in the five core areas, which are math, science, history, English, foreign language, and then we also weight classes that are honors+ level.

—*Michael G. Tarantino, Assistant Director of Undergraduate Admissions,*
Sacred Heart University, Connecticut

Feedback

Students who preferred the SAT claim that the math was more conceptual and therefore focused their efforts on mastering vocabulary for critical reading. For them, it was easier to prepare for just two content areas. Those who did not prefer the SAT felt constrained by time limits, number of sections, and number of questions per section. They also did not appreciate being penalized for wrong answers, which made them afraid to guess.

Students who preferred the ACT felt that there was less stress in completing four larger areas of testing, including English, reading, math, and science reasoning. They felt the math section reflected more recently learned concepts and was therefore easier. All students appreciated the lack of penalty for wrong answers, which allowed them to guess when they otherwise did not know the answer.

Both the SAT and the ACT include timed, prompted writing assessments. The ACT charges an additional fee for this option at the time of registration. It's important to complete this section to the best of your ability. Some colleges use this score to determine admission decisions, some use it to determine your placement for English courses, and other don't use it at all. No matter which schools you are considering, it's in your best interest to take this section seriously and do well.

If you find it difficult to determine which test will earn you a higher score, then you should take both tests during your junior year. After receiving and reviewing your scores, you can choose to study and focus on either type of test during senior year.

Tip

Most juniors choose to take the SAT in May and receive their scores via Internet in June. You then have the opportunity to take the SAT again in November as a senior. By that time, you have compiled your initial list of schools and know specific admission test averages and requirements. You still have time to increase your efforts and level of preparation for the exam, which may include online tutorials, a prep course, or a one-on-one tutor.

The college application process was full of stress. In my opinion, the worst part was the time that it consumed. The fact that I did not take my SATs until December 4th truly hurt my ability to apply. I felt that the essay was the easiest part. At the end of the process, I'm hoping to hear good news. I would like to play baseball in college as well. The whole college application experience was one of the most stressful points in my life.

—Tyler B., high school senior

For Parents

If a student does not take a college admission test during his or her junior year, it can be difficult to estimate the scores, which makes it challenging to determine which schools to consider. Because November is the traditional test date for seniors, scores will not be available until December, and most college applications need to be completed by Thanksgiving or December break at the latest. If necessary, there are additional testing dates in September or October for consideration.

The results on the standardized tests are one factor that determines your chance of acceptance. It's not the most important factor, but it can be in the top three. Ideally, you should take both exams at least once. If you don't achieve the needed scores at first, there must be opportunity to retake the tests.

For Parents

It's very important for you to support your student during the preparation for these tests. These are not IQ tests. There are strategies and tips that your student needs to know in order to do well. Also, most students are not disciplined enough to structure a study regimen. It is up to you to provide whatever support you can. This may include motivational and financial support for test registrations, online tutorials, prep courses, or tutoring.

Most universities hold the GPA and coursework as the top two factors, and then the SAT/ACT would be tied with them at most schools as well, except for those schools who are test-optional (like us). The ranking is becoming less relevant as many high schools no longer calculate class rank.

—Michael G. Tarantino, Assistant Director of Undergraduate Admissions, Sacred Heart University, Connecticut

For Parents

You will need to provide a credit card for the secure Internet registration for college admission tests, as well as application fees. If you prefer another method of payment, please consult your student's guidance counselor.

For Parents

Active participation and monitoring of your student's study plan, benchmarks, and test dates are beneficial. Knowledge and communication create a shared outcome for you and your student—one as test taker, the other as cheerleader, both with the highest expectations.

Official score reports must be sent to each school, often for an additional fee. If you plan to take advantage of early application deadlines, you are required to submit your documents by a specific date in October or November. Accordingly, the latest test date that you would be able to sit for would be in September or early October.

For a typical regular admission deadline of January 1, you may register to take the December test dates for either the SAT or ACT exam. Results are typically available online three weeks after the test date. Check with your guidance counselor for his or her recommendations.

Don't forget that if finances are an issue, test-taking agencies offer fee waivers to qualified applicants. Please contact your guidance counselor for details. In addition, there are many low- and no-cost options for test-preparation resources, which include College Board and ACT Student websites, Naviance software modules, online tutorials, and public/high school library reference books.

Super Score is a great policy that's beneficial to all students; check with admissions to see whether colleges you are considering embrace this philosophy. Don't be nervous that college admission officers will see your worst scores. Super Score allows them to use the highest math and English/critical reading scores from *all* of your scores to calculate your best total or composite score. It may even include your best score for one section of your ACT and another high score from your SAT, out of all the times you took the tests.

> *Applying to colleges was very stressful. It was a very involved process that took a lot of time to perfect. I had to make sure that I had everything I needed and that all of my information was filled in correctly. I must have spent at least an hour just staring at my high school transcript and everything I filled in on the SUNY website, making sure all the classes and grades I filled in were correct. My college essay was another thing I stressed about. I made changes and improvements all the time and tried to make sure it was a great essay. Once I was done with everything I needed to do, I felt very relieved. Knowing I had one less thing to worry about felt great. Now I am waiting to hear back from the colleges I applied to, and I can't wait to get the letters, whether they are acceptances or rejections, in the mail.*

> **—Shannon D., high school senior**

Cautionary Tale

Some very large college systems don't have enough admissions-office staff to personally review all admissions materials. These schools rely on specialized software that recommends an admissions decision based solely on objective factors, standardized admission test scores, coursework, and grades. Letters of recommendations, college essays, and summaries of extracurricular activities are not accepted or considered in the process. An example is the highly acclaimed City of New York's Higher Education (CUNY) system at www.cuny.edu. Some students appreciate the ease of this application process, whereas others feel cheated by not being permitted to submit supplemental application materials.

Test Registration

You can complete SAT registration on College Board's website at www.collegeboard.org. You will need to navigate to the SAT homepage, follow the links to sign up for an account, and complete registration.

Students generally prefer to take the exam at their own high school or one with which they are familiar; however, most high schools are not listed as an SAT testing location on every testing date. The most popular dates to take the test are May (for juniors) and November (for seniors). Make sure to register early, because some locations reach maximum test-taking capacity and additional registrants are diverted to surrounding schools.

ACT registration is done through the www.actstudent.org website, where you will be prompted to create a student account. Similarly to the SAT, you must select an available testing site for your test date.

Point to Ponder

Some schools offer preparation courses and tutorials specifically geared toward only one test—for example, the SAT. To prepare for the science and higher-level math on the ACT, you may need to seek out other methods and resources.

SAT Subject Tests

SAT Subject Tests, or SAT IIs, are required or recommended by select colleges as part of the application process. These hour-long tests are content-specific, so students should take these tests in May of the year they complete the coursework. Therefore, if you plan to apply to highly selective or competitive colleges, you need to prepare, register, and take these SAT Subject Tests in tenth, eleventh or twelfth grade.

Note

When you register for either the SAT or the ACT, you are awarded four free score reports. Please take advantage of this offer. If you wait to order the reports until after you receive your scores, you'll be charged at least $10 for each official score report requested. There is no downside to taking advantage of four free reports. Remember, colleges consider only your highest score for each section on any test date, and admissions officers don't hold poor scores against you.

College Board offers these 20 tests across five subject areas, which include history, math, science, English, and foreign languages. You can register for these exams through your College Board account at www.collegeboard.org or at http://sat.collegeboard.org/about-tests/sat-subject-tests, and you can take up to three SAT Subject Tests on one day. Make a point to consult with your guidance counselor to get direction as to which tests to take and when.

Note

Only upon finalizing the list of schools you are considering will you know whether you need to submit SAT Subject Tests. It's better to have this testing requirement completed when content is fresh in your mind. Don't wait until senior year; you already have enough to do!

Right about now, you may start to feel the pressures of having to complete your college applications. Don't panic! Stay focused. Set a schedule to prepare for your college admission tests. Maintain your good grades. Breathe.

Keep reading this text, following the timeline in Appendix C, and completing steps and worksheets as listed. Enjoy your senior year. Breathe.

Ideally, you should begin the application process by September 15th and have all requirements completed and submitted by November 20th—just in time to enjoy Thanksgiving dinner, stress-free. Breathe.

When evaluating applications, the components that are more important are coursework, GPA, SAT/ACT, extracurricular activities, essay, and interest in the college (how much contact the student has initiated). Legacy and sibling connections are important and at times weigh heavily in the process.

—Emmanuel Cruz, Admissions Counselor, Hartwick College, New York

Chapter 7
And Three More

*We track **everything**. Every email, phone call, Facebook visit, and Twitter tweets. They all count! Campus visits and college fairs, too.*

—**Michael G. Tarantino, Assistant Director of Undergraduate Admissions, Sacred Heart University, Connecticut**

The remaining parts of the college application are more subjective, allowing for self-expression and interpretation. You have a lot of control and input into your activity sheet or resume, letters of recommendation, and college essay. They may take some time to finalize, but once you complete these remaining components, you can use them for each college's application.

Extracurricular Activity Sheet/Resume

Colleges earn their reputations on the success, activism, and accomplishments of their graduates. It seems likely that a student who has been very active in high school should continue to be very active during college. And in the future, these employed, actively engaged men and women will go forward in life to excel and prosper while sharing the rewards of their involvement with those in their communities and beyond.

College admissions committees are eager to see you interact with others and grow beyond the classroom in long-term, organized commitments. However, this is not about joining every club and volunteering at every charitable event in town during your senior year; it's about the quality and depth of your involvement.

Bottom line: Colleges want active citizens on their campus. They don't want students who sometimes make it to class and then go back to their dorm rooms to nap and watch TV all day.

There are no "best" extracurricular activities; just do what you enjoy and do it with energy and passion, taking advantage of any leadership opportunities that you encounter along the way. Commit to a variety during your high school years, or commit to few regularly and consistently. Part-time employment, sports, clubs, the arts and performance, community service, or personal hobbies are all wonderful examples of your involvement.

For Parents

In this day and age, most students are bombarded with experiences, activities, and memberships, plus most high schools now have graduation requirements for community-service hours. Your student's challenge may not be not having enough involvement for a solid college application, but rather being unable to properly document and describe all of it. This is where you can be of great assistance. Hopefully, you saved all records that can assist in creating an activity sheet. This activity sheet should include the names, dates, roles, purposes, and awards for all extracurricular events through the high school years, both school-sponsored and outside.

If you weren't able to document these activities at the time, you can still help by recalling details or by contacting coaches, advisors, leaders, supervisors, teachers, and so on to obtain the necessary information.

After being so actively engaged in life and community, you must frame your experiences in a manner that is easy to read and recognized. The activity sheet takes time to complete; you may have to start and stop many times before you are finished. It is vital to include accurate, detailed information. If you need to, contact your guidance counselor, former coaches and teammates, advisors, mentors, and others to obtain the correct information.

Word processing is equally important—presentation counts. Most likely you or your guidance counselor will be uploading or attaching this document via the Internet, so use an easy-to-read font in an appropriate size. Don't be in a rush to submit this document; make sure it's well formatted and contains detailed, accurate information.

Please be sure that your full name, address, and phone number appear on each page. Also, note that it's not advisable or necessary to include your Social Security number as identification. To guard against identity theft, most schools no longer use Social Security numbers on documents or identification cards.

Point to Ponder

Acronyms (initials) are commonly used to describe clubs and activities in your town. When you send your activity sheet to colleges in another state, admissions officers may not easily recognize or understand the abbreviations. Make sure you spell out activity and team names while offering descriptions of the organization when necessary. You don't want anyone to be confused about the wonderful things you have been doing these last few years.

The following is a sample activity sheet compiled with a variety of different types of activities for both males and females. Use it to develop the layout and descriptions for your extracurricular activities and accomplishments, noting the simple, direct wording and format.

Reference Sheet C:
Activity Sheet—Completed Sample

Michael Kate Student

Street Address
Town, ST Zip
Phone with Area Code

SPORTS

Team Name	Position(s) Held	Dates of Participation	Team Record/Tournaments/ Awards/Leadership/Individual Accomplishments
Varsity Cheerleading	Back Spotter & Base	2012–2014	**Captain (2013–2014)** Cheered at all varsity football and basketball games.
Varsity Competition Cheerleading Team	Back Spotter & Base	2012–2014	**Captain (2013–2014)** Competed in LICCA competitions. Earned first place at Regional Championships.
JV Football	Right Guard	Fall 2013 & 2014	2013 Team Record: 5-3 **Most Outstanding Defensive Lineman award** (2013).
Varsity Hockey	Goalie	Winter 2012 & 2013	2012 Team Record: 17-9-1
JV Soccer	Midfielder	Fall 2014	Team Record: 13-1
Varsity Track and Field	Member	Winter 2009	2010 Record: 5-1 Second place in division.
Winter Varsity Track	Long-Distance Runner	Winter 2012	Competed in 300m and 600m races.

Clubs

Club Name	Position(s) Held	Dates of Membership	Goals/Responsibilites/ Leadership
Cantante	Member	2012–2014	Highly select vocal group that performs extremely difficult pieces of music, sometimes *a capella*.
Century Club	Member	2011	Completed more than 100 hours of community service.
Class of 2014	Member	2011–2014	Organized and participated in fundraising events to support class activities.
DECA Marketing Club	Member	2012–2013	Attended all meetings. Participated in competitive events. Earned second place in entrepreneurship district competition.
DECA School Store	Manager	2012–2013	Managed scheduling and inventory. Calculated inventory orders. Operated cash register. Processed cash transactions.
Earth and Outdoors Club	Member	2013–2014	Attended all meetings. Cleaned and maintained local community and beaches. Helped institute school-wide recycling program.
Environmental Club	Member	2008–2009	Attended all meetings. Brainstormed ideas and programs to promote "greener" lifestyle. Participated in cleanup events for the environment, school, and surrounding community.
Future Business Leaders of America	Member	2010–2014	**President (2013–2014)** Attended all meetings. Participated in resume workshop and business-card workshop. Organized fundraisers and field trips.
Peer Mediation	Nominated Member	2010–2012	Selected and trained as a peer mediator. Assisted classmates in conflict resolution.
Student Senate	Member	2011–2013	Participated in community service events, including various fundraisers and annual Christmas party for disabled children.
Vocal Movement	Member	2010–2012	Performed with highly competitive, select vocal/dance troupe. Traveled to performance venues, including Disney World, Washington D.C., and Canada.
Yearbook Club	Vice President	2013–2014	Designed page layout and theme for annual yearbook. Photographed clubs and sports teams. Collected and managed photos and data from members.

Activities

Organization Name	Activity Name	Dates of Membership/ Participation	Description/Responsibilites
Catastrophe	Founding Member/ Bass Guitarist	2010–present	Practice with band regularly. Perform at various venues, including street fairs and fundraisers.
Elite Gymnastics	Gymnastics Training	2003–present	Attend tumbling classes. Learn new techniques and practice good form.
B'nai Israel Temple	Youth Basketball	2010–2012	Attended all practices. Competed in weekly games.
WHS Orchestra	Cellist	2009–2013	Attended weekly lessons. Performed in all concerts.

Work Experience

Company Name	Position(s) Held	Dates of Employment	Job Responsibilites/ Recognition
Community Learning Group	Program Aide	September 2011–present	Supervise children with developmental disabilities at after-school program. Assist teacher with lessons, crafts, and activities.
Martin Drug Stores	Cashier	September 2009–present	Provide customer service. Operate cash register. Process cash and credit transactions. Stock merchandise. Arrange product display. Clean and maintain store. Collect carts.
Great Bay YMCA	Jr. Camp Counselor	Summer 2012 and 2013	Supervised 15 children, ages 7 and 8. Assisted campers with sports, crafts, and activities.
Self-Employed	Tutor	September 2010–present	Tutored fifth- and seventh-grade students in all subject areas.
Slices & Ices	Cashier/Cook	Summer 2011 and 2012	Provided customer service. Operated cash register. Processed cash and credit transactions. Prepared food and drinks. Cleaned and maintained counter and dining area.
Smith Family	Babysitter	Summer 2011	Supervised two children, ages 8 and 10. Prepared snacks and meals. Assisted children with homework and activities.

Awards and Honors

School/ Organization Name	Name of Award	Date of Award	Description of Achievement
National Honor Society	Inducted Member	September 2011– present	Recognized for outstanding academic achievement, community service, and teacher recommendation.
New York State Business and Marketing Honor Society	Inducted Member	September 2011– present	Recognized for outstanding academic achievement in business-education classes, community service, and teacher recommendation.
National English Honor Society	Inducted Member	September 2011– present	Recognized for outstanding academic achievement in English, community service, and teacher recommendation.
West High School	Principal's List	September 2009– present	Awarded to students who earn an overall average of 90 or above.
West High School Math Department	Math Honor Roll	September 2009– present	Awarded to students who earn a 90 or above average in math.
West High School Health Education Department	Health Student of the Month	April 2010	Recognized for high achievement and participation in health.
West High School Math Department	Departmental Scholar	June 2011	Recognized for high achievement and participation in math.
FBLA Tax Day Invitational Competition	First Place in Accounting	April 2010	Earned first place in regional competition.

Volunteerism

Organization Name	Program	Date(s) of Service	Services Provided/ Responsibilites
WATCH US Daycare	Program Aide	September 2010–June 2011	Provided children with snacks and drinks. Assisted children with homework. Supervised children during playtime.
Class of 2015	Parents' Night Out	December 2013	Planned activities and supervised children. Raised funds for class activities.
National Honor Society	Tutor	September 2012–June 2013	Tutored fifth-grade student in math. Tutored sixth-grade student in reading.
National Honor Society	Open House at West High School	September 2014	Greeted and guided parents to classrooms during community event.
National Honor Society	Annual Halloween Haunt	October 2013 and 2014	Set up, decorated, and participated in a Halloween event for elementary school children. Donated decorations and candy for the event.
St. Joseph's R.C. Church	Vacation Bible School Counselor	Summer 2014	Supervised 10 campers, ages 9 and 10. Assisted children with Bible lessons, crafts, and activities.
Student Senate	Invisible Children	Fall 2014	Sold bracelets to raise money for children in Uganda.
West Town Beautification Committee	Clean Up	Spring 2014	Cleaned and maintained surrounding community, including painting fences and planting flowers.
West High School World Language Department	Language Outreach Program	October 2013– May 2013	Planned lessons and taught Italian to elementary school children each week.
County Conference Cheerleading Association	Youth League Head Coach	Fall 2014	Taught fourth and fifth graders a competition routine. Coached sideline cheers at youth league football games.
West Town Soccer Club	Indoor Tournament	November 2010	Assisted with player/team registration. Processed registration fee transactions.

You can use Worksheet 9 to draft your own activity sheet. When you're finished, make sure the layout and spacing are even and that you have been consistent throughout the document. If you need assistance in the final phase, especially proofreading, ask for it. Many teachers and other adults are willing to help you achieve your dreams.

You will also use this activity sheet as an attachment for scholarship and grant applications. And don't forget to include it when asking a teacher, coach, or supervisor to write a letter of recommendation. This allows the letter-writer to author a detailed, engaging, vibrant letter to support your admission to the colleges of your choice.

Worksheet 9:
Draft Activity Sheet

Your Name

Street Address
Town, ST Zip
Phone with Area Code

SPORTS

Team Name	Position(s) Held	Dates of Participation	Team Record/Tournaments/ Awards/Leadership/Individual Accomplishments

Activities

Organization Name	Activity Name	Dates of Membership/ Participation	Description/Responsibilites

Work Experience

Company Name	Position(s) Held	Dates of Employment	Job Responsibilites/ Recognition

Awards and Honors

School/ Organization Name	Name of Award	Date of Award	Description of Achievement

Volunteerism

Organization Name	Program	Date(s) of Service	Services Provided/ Responsibilites

Letters of Recommendation

Throughout life, it's important to maintain connections with others who will speak highly of you and your work. College admissions committees look forward to reading these letters written on your behalf. At your age, your network can include teachers, administrators, coaches, advisors, church or religious leaders, supervisors, and so on.

Choose people who can share great details about your wonderful characteristics and accomplishments. It's advisable to ask two or three people to write letters of recommendation for you. One should be a teacher from your junior year who can write about your excellent attendance, participation, and effort level. Another could be someone to write about your participation and leadership in a specific sport, club, civic organization, or activity.

> **Note**
>
> Some teachers will share the letter they write with you. Others will keep a copy on file while independently sending your letters directly to the colleges. The Common Application requires you to complete a Privacy (FERPA) Notice to officially waive or not waive your rights to see these letters written about you, even after you matriculate (enroll) at school.

Remember to include a copy of your completed activity sheet when requesting letters of recommendation. Even if your activity sheet isn't 100 percent complete, it's a great idea to include it with your requests. No doubt your letter-writer will be quite impressed with your involvement in and out of school. You should also give a copy of the activity sheet to your guidance counselor to keep on file and assist him/her in authoring a separate letter that details your growth and experience throughout high school.

No teacher writes a negative letter of recommendation. However, it isn't a good sign if your chosen person responds with, "Are you sure you want me to write this letter? Don't you have anyone else you'd rather ask?" It's a clear indication that there are some misunderstandings about the quality of your work and level of maturity. At that point, you really must consider whether there's someone else you would rather ask.

*Teachers are writing the right things when they really have a connection with the student, but we still see a lot of generic letters from teachers. Students should ask teachers who **really** know them well and with whom students have had a great connection on an academic and social level as well.*

—Michael G. Tarantino, Assistant Director of Undergraduate Admissions, Sacred Heart University, Connecticut

Caution

Some students enjoy the antics of a "class clown," whereas many teachers look forward to the end of the semester. Conversely, some students enjoy the anonymity of not participating or engaging the teacher during class. Both of these types of students may feel desperate when deciding whom to ask for a letter of recommendation.

It's important for students to know early on in high school (and in life) that networking and interpersonal relationships are vital to future success.

The letter in Reference Sheet D provides an example of how to request a letter of recommendation. Make sure you provide quality information and specific instructions to your letter-writers. You should also be polite and appreciative of their efforts and support.

You can use Worksheet 10 as a template to request letters of recommendations from your network. Keep a dated copy of the request for yourself. You can email or mail the request, but it's always best to ask in person.

For letter recommendations, we are looking for honesty from teachers and guidance counselors. If the teacher knows that student is struggling in class, it would be good for the teacher to acknowledge it but explain why the student is going to be a good fit at our college. For guidance counselors, we know they want the student to get into college, but from their end we would like to know which personal traits will ensure this student will succeed (retention-wise) at the school.

—Emmanuel Cruz, Admissions Counselor, Hartwick College, New York

---

Reference Sheet D: Sample Request for Letter of Recommendation

September 20, 2014

Dear Ms. Portnoy,

How are you? As you know, it's the beginning of my senior year and time to start the college application process. I would like to ask you to please write a letter of recommendation for me. Since entering high school, I have been a student in your class for:

- College Accounting—Senior Year
- Web Design—Sophomore Year
- Computer Essentials—Freshman Year

Additionally, I have volunteered for the last two years at the Celebrate Education event and participated in the FBLA Tax Day Competitions. For the past three years, I have been a member in good standing in the Business and Marketing Honor Society and DECA. I plan to major in accounting, eventually earning my Certified Public Accounting license.

I have attached a draft version of my activity sheet for your review. It contains details about my involvement in activities both in and out of school, as well as the awards that I have won.

- ☒ Since I don't have a finalized list of colleges that I plan to apply to, you can address the letter to the Admissions Committee. I expect to need **10** copies of this letter.

- ☐ I will be providing you with pre-addressed, stamped envelopes, so that you will be able to directly mail the letters to the colleges.

- ☒ I plan to use the Common Application website for my applications and will "invite" you to upload your letter directly to the site. Please keep an eye out for the email.

- ☐ I may choose to participate in the Immediate Decision Day process, which requires the letters to be presented directly to the admissions officer at the time of my appointment. I will also provide envelopes properly labeled for this purpose.

- ☒ I plan to apply before the Early Action deadline. All of my materials, including your letter, need to be completed and submitted by **November 15th**.

And finally, can you please send a copy of the letter to my guidance counselor, **Ms. Kirby**, so she can keep it in my file for future use.

I greatly appreciate your time and effort to write this letter. It has been a great experience to have you as a teacher. If you would like to contact me or need additional information, you can email me at student@email.com.

Thank you!

A. Student

Worksheet 10: Draft Request for Letter of Recommendation

DATE

Dear _____,

How are you? As you know, it is the beginning of my senior year and time to start the college application process. I would like to ask you to write a letter of recommendation for me. Since entering high school, I have been a student in your class for:

Additionally,

_____
_____
_____

I have attached a draft version of my activity sheet for your review. It contains details about my involvement in activities both in and out of school, as well as the awards that I have won.

☐ Since I don't have a finalized list of colleges that I plan to apply to, you can address the letter to the Admissions Committee. I expect to need __ copies of this letter.

☐ I will be providing you with pre-addressed, stamped envelopes, so that you will be able to directly mail the letters to the colleges.

☐ I plan to use the Common Application website for my applications and will "invite" you to upload your letter directly to the site. Please keep an eye out for the email.

☐ I may choose to participate in the Immediate Decision Day process, which requires the letters to be presented directly to the admissions officer at the time of my appointment. I will also provide envelopes properly labeled for this purpose.

☐ I plan to apply before the Early Action deadline. All of my materials, including your letter, need to be completed and submitted by _____.

And finally, can you please send a copy of the letter to my guidance counselor, _____, so he/she can keep it in my file for future use.

I greatly appreciate your time and effort to write this letter. It has been a great experience to have you as a teacher. If you would like to contact me or need additional information, you can email me at _____.

Thank you!

_____

After you've requested your letters, referring to Worksheet 6: School Services Questionnaire, determine who is responsible for mailing them to the colleges. In some cases, teachers submit their letters to your guidance counselor. The letters are placed in your file, and will be photocopied and sent to each school with other supporting materials. Otherwise, the teacher mails them directly, so you'll need to provide addressed, stamped envelopes to each letter-writer for your application with each school. Purchase a box of #10 business envelopes at your local office supply store, if necessary.

> **Note**
>
> Most word processing programs have a feature for printing envelopes using your home printer. It's important to verify the correct mailing address for these letters. It may be a different address from where you send the main application or fees. Check the application instructions or Undergraduate Admissions link on the official school website.
>
> Microsoft Word's envelope template is located under Mailings (tab), Envelopes (icon). For future use, it's best to save the file for each admissions department address. Often an additional envelope may be necessary.

Colleges are consistently moving toward the electronic submission of all forms, including letters of recommendation. This process requires the teacher to write the letter of recommendation and upload the final version through an Internet portal or website, which allows for immediate transmission and receipt.

For example, when you use the Common Application at www.commonapp.org to apply to college, there is an option that allows you to "invite" an official who can access the portal for completing and uploading the recommendation forms. These "officials" include your guidance counselor and other teachers and professionals of your choice. It's crucial that you have the correct email address for each of these participants. You should still request a letter using the template in Worksheet 10 and include your activity sheet. Just because the process is completed via the Internet doesn't mean any of *your* requirements have changed. You still need to provide your letter-writers with information to write an awesome letter.

> **Note**
>
> For many years, admissions departments across the country were responsible for processing, sorting, and analyzing hundreds of thousands of pieces of paper. The process has now been digitized. You and every other applicant will have an electronic file that includes uploaded or scanned application forms, letters, transcripts, activity sheets, essays, and supplemental documents. The files are then shared and reviewed in their digital form by the admissions officers and committees.

College Essays

Many students are intimidated by the idea of writing a college essay. In truth, they shouldn't be. The college essay is usually limited to 500 words or fewer, which amounts to two pages, double-spaced. Throughout high school, students are required to do a lot more writing than this.

College admissions officers are looking to read an interesting essay that shows growth and awareness, attention to detail, and strong writing skills.

Choosing the right topic is often the most difficult part of writing the college essay. Once you have done so, the words, emotions, and insights will flow easily. Truthfully, most students write too much, going on and on but not really saying anything. Most college applications, including the Common Application at www.commonapp.org, give you a choice of three or more topics, plus the option of choosing your own topic.

Interesting topics that show growth and awareness reflect maturity. Choosing an appropriate topic shows your individuality and awareness of life's opportunities, which may include hope, happiness, and experience.

If you are looking for more inspiration or assistance in selecting a topic, use the Internet to search for "college essay topics." The results often list more than 100 topics that have been used previously or required by colleges across the U.S. Perusing this listing may awaken you to a brilliant essay opportunity that you've never considered.

Attention to detail requires proofreading for spelling, grammar, and structure. You should ask at least three adults to proofread your essay. Hopefully one of them is a favorite English teacher, who has experience providing feedback and identifying areas to improve. If you are including the name of a specific college in your essay, make sure to spell the school name correctly and change it when required.

Strong writing skills include the ability to write coherent thoughts within organized paragraphs, using active voice, proper grammar, and age-appropriate vocabulary and expressions. No slang or texting abbreviations allowed.

---

*Write something **positive**.... Admissions reps read over 30 essays a day during the application season, and all of the depressing essays start to drain us. Avoid the three D's: divorce, disaster, and death. There are so many stories about someone overcoming the death of their grandmother that it starts to wear thin. The essay is important, and making sure the right school is written and there are no spelling/grammatical errors are crucial.*

**—Michael G. Tarantino, Assistant Director of Undergraduate Admissions,
Sacred Heart University, Connecticut**

Tip

Most admissions officers can easily identify an essay that has *not* been written by a teen. It's wonderful to get assistance and guidance from the adults in your life, but it's totally unnecessary to give up your own opportunity for expression.

Ms. Portnoy was extremely helpful in my college application process. I had to rely on myself to complete my applications in a timely fashion and that nobody would do it for me. Overall, the college application process was simple; however, writing my essay was time consuming and stressful because you have the opportunity to write about anything. Choosing a topic was difficult, and reflecting on my life made it seem so boring. But eventually I constructed a well-written essay, and to my surprise, an admissions counselor complimented me on it.

—Emily A., high school senior

Other Items to Include

According to admissions counselors, they enjoy receiving additional materials in the form of videos, artwork, and creative pieces that reflect positively on the applicant. Make sure that it's appropriate, meaning that you would share it with your grandmother, too.

Depending on your intended major, you may be required to submit portfolios or perform auditions. These items and performances are presented after the general college application materials and fees are submitted and reviewed, usually in the winter or spring of senior year.

Don't forget to maintain frequent contact and communication with the college admissions representatives for your hometown, especially for feedback and support during the application process. These are the same professionals who present informational sessions at your high school and man the tables during college fairs. Make sure to keep their contact information readily available.

PART IV
Schools and Applications

When people ask you about applying to college, they're referring to the number and names of schools you are trying to get accepted at and the requirements that go with it. As you have seen, a lot of preparation and planning come before this point, if you do it with thought and intention.

Even though you have been working on it and toward it the entire time, you are now ready to finalize your list of schools and begin the physical process of completing applications, which is actually a separate process within the process. You are on your way!

Chapter 8
Do You Have What It Takes?

Don't stress!!! People stress out about this process, and the ball is really in your court. Every college wants you. The pressure is really on us to impress you enough to choose our school.

—Michael G. Tarantino, Assistant Director of Undergraduate Admissions, Sacred Heart University, Connecticut

The good news is that there are plenty of schools where you will be accepted. The bad news is that there is no way to guarantee that you'll get into one particular school. There have been a few sad stories over the years where students didn't get into any of their top-choice schools.

With no guarantee, the approach in this matter is fundamental: to make sure *you* have *options*. By springtime, you should have acceptances to many schools from your list and be able to make a final decision based on location, cost, prestige, or any other factor important to *you*.

One of the simplest ways to analyze your chances for acceptance is to compare your GPA and college admissions test scores to each school's average. You can get this information from schools' official websites, Naviance, or your guidance counselor. I recommend these two Internet sites to find data for all schools:

College Board's Big Future at www.bigfuture.collegeboard.org college planning tool provides necessary information used to further categorize your choice of colleges. Search for a school, then navigate to the Applying tab, where you will find links to Application Requirements, Academics, and SAT & ACT Scores. By logging in to your College Board account, you can save colleges to your list for future use and comparison.

College Navigator at www.nces.ed.gov/collegenavigator is another resource available to assist students, parents, and guidance counselors. It is a free tool offered by the National Center for Education Statistics. Because it's a government website, you won't encounter any advertisements or diversions during your research.

The layout for College Navigator is very straightforward. You can search for schools based on specific criteria, including name, location, degrees awarded, institution type, tuition costs, undergraduate enrollment, housing, campus setting, percentage of applicants accepted, test scores, athletic teams, religious affiliation, and/or specialized mission. Each school's profile offers comprehensive data according to category, which you can expand and collapse as necessary, all on one page.

Use the data available in Admissions to conduct your analysis: The Percent Admitted statistic will assist you in categorizing a school as Safety, Target, Reach, or Shot in the Dark, and the Test Scores Percentiles report midrange scores for students who were accepted by and enrolled at the school.

After you view a college's profile, you can add it to your favorites for later use. For instance, you can compare, side by side, up to four colleges in the areas of estimated student expenses, financial aid, net price, enrollment, admissions, retention, and graduation rates. In addition, you have the option to print the comparison or import it to an MS Excel spreadsheet. If you would like to save your results, a link can be sent to your email address.

Using your academic record and test scores, along with the resources listed above, complete Worksheet 11: Categorizing Schools to help you fine tune and trim your Worksheet 8: Initial List of Schools to a manageable list of schools to which you plan to apply.

Include all of the schools you selected when researching majors and add three or four schools from your state university system, any schools you have been dreaming about, and the schools that your grandpa and auntie want you to attend.

Point to Ponder

Most people think of safety schools as those you are assured of getting accepted at. I recommend having financial safety schools from your state system and close-to-home safety schools as well. You never know how your life circumstances will change by next spring.

My college application process was a bit confusing at first, but Ms. Portnoy helped a lot. I would recommend it to anyone applying to colleges during their senior year. I had the most trouble with finding time to complete all the applications. There were so many questions, and every college was just a little bit different, so I couldn't just copy and paste from college to college. They all wanted different information and essay topics. I am done with the majority of the work, and now I'm waiting for responses. My parents helped me a lot, but much of what I had to do I had to do by myself.

—**Brian C., high school senior**

PRINT THIS!

Worksheet 11:
Categorizing Schools: Safety, Target, Reach, Shot in the Dark

Your Scores:

GPA after 11th Grade	Testing Date	SAT Critical Reading	SAT Math	ACT Composite	ACT English	ACT Math
	1st Attempt					
Based on 100-point scale	2nd Attempt					
	3rd Attempt					
Converted to 4.0 scale	SuperScore*					

* Identify and circle your highest scores in each section to determine your SuperScore.

Target School: Your test scores and GPA fall with the range; you meet the stated academic requirements.[1]

Safety School: Your test scores and GPA are at the high end of the range; you meet or exceed academic requirements.[1]

Reach School: You do not meet one or more of the requirements but may feel that you can still qualify or impress the admissions committee.

Shot-in-the-Dark School: You do not meet the requirements but would like to apply anyway.

---

[1] When applying to highly selective schools, even though you meet the stated requirements you still may not be accepted. No acceptance at this caliber of school is guaranteed.

School Information and Statistics

PRINT THIS!

School Name	Official Website Address	Percent of Students Accepted	Median GPA	Average SAT Range (Critical Reading/Math)	Average ACT range (Composite)	Safety/Target/ Reach/ Shot in the Dark

Point to Ponder

It may sound strange, but you don't want to be accepted at all the schools where you apply—that would be playing it too safe. You want to reach, to stretch the boundaries, to see what you're capable of. You want to know you didn't sell yourself short.

Guidance counselors can assist you in categorizing schools based on their experience with previous applicants and direct knowledge of your academic records and characteristics.

College Websites

You must become familiar with the official websites of schools where you plan to apply. You should visit them often, sign up to receive additional information, and stay informed of open house and special events. Unfortunately, no two websites have the same layout or design. Like a detective, you need to look for the appropriate links. Start by looking for Prospective Students, Freshmen, Admissions, or Undergraduate Admissions.

PRINT THIS! When you arrive at the Undergraduate Admissions homepage, you can usually locate a link to the school's admissions requirements, which detail required high school courses, admission test scores, and required GPA, as well as required SAT Subject Tests, if applicable. Colleges often provide a Quick Facts webpage where this data is summarized.

The link to Programs of Study or Majors is equally as important because not every major or program of study is offered at every college. Some students are disappointed to find that a favorite school doesn't support the intended major for their career path.

To assist prospective students in their research, New York's SUNY system offers a Program Search at https://www.suny.edu/student/search_programs/currfd_oas_main.cfm to easily identify which of their 64 campuses offers specific programs and majors.

PRINT THIS! College websites post the most up-to-date statistics based on the previous year's freshman class. For example, the SUNY system publishes Admission Quick Facts and Information Summary for their university centers and colleges at www.suny.edu/student/forms.cfm which details average SAT and ACT scores as well as the GPA of admitted students. It also includes a listing of which NCAA division sports are available at each campus.

PRINT THIS! Similarly, Penn State posts their admission statistics at http://admissions.psu.edu/academics/majors/requirements/50percent. The California State University system posts their Eligibility Index at http://www.csumentor.edu/planning/high_school/grades_tests.asp. Rutgers, the State University of New Jersey, lists the entrance requirements to their three campuses and competitive majors/programs at http://admissions.rutgers.edu/ApplyNow/MoreForFirstYearApplicants/EntranceRequirements.aspx.

How Many Schools?

When you're ready to start accessing applications, you should have a perfect mix of 6 to 10 schools with great reputations, varying costs of attendance, and different locations and settings.

You can choose to apply to fewer or more schools; it is totally up to you and your parents, considering that each school charges an application fee of between $35 and $100. But think BIG PICTURE: You are about to spend $50,000 to $200,000 on a college education, so maybe spending $500 to make sure you have the best options to choose from isn't such a waste of money. It's up to you.

> **Point to Ponder**
>
> Any state university system is partially funded by taxpayer dollars, so the tuition is cheaper for students who are residents of that state. There are specific requirements to prove state residency—it depends on the rules for each state system. For some states, owning property is enough to establish residency. In other states, you must graduate from a high school in the state. Check with the admissions office for guidelines.

Traditionally, private colleges and universities, which are not supported by tax dollars, are more expensive than their public counterparts. However, do not rule out colleges based on cost alone. In the spring, after you complete your financial-aid forms, after you receive your admission decision, you'll receive a financial-aid package that is specific to each school.

We track interest in our school through the following ways:

- *Every inquiry card filled out*
- *Showing up to a high school visit*
- *College fair visits*
- *Thank-you emails/letters*
- *Parent phone calls/emails*
- *Student phone calls/reply emails*
- *Visits on campus*
- *Off-campus interviews*
- *Off-campus receptions*
- *Alumni referrals/recommendations*
- *Facebook/Twitter inquires, Facebook accounts, and Internet searches*

—Emmanuel Cruz, Admissions Counselor, Hartwick College, New York

Financial-aid packages are based on the cost of each school. Most likely, you will receive more financial aid to support that dream of attending a very expensive school if you want to do so. Also, many private colleges have very generous alumni who support and endow current students with scholarships. But you need to get accepted to schools before turning any down, so keep moving forward with the process.

Getting Feedback

Now that you have analyzed the admissions requirements of 15 to 20 colleges that have a strong program for your future studies, you need to get input from the experts. These experts include your parents, who know you and may be helping to finance your dreams; your guidance counselor, who knows your academic record and the history of admission decisions at your high school; and knowledgeable extended family and friends who understand your intended program of study, the industry, and outlook/expectations.

> **Point to Ponder**
>
> Don't be afraid to tell your story. Be proud of your plan and share it with all who are interested. You'll be surprised by insights and ideas that others share. Life can be inspiring and complicated; learn from others, or at least accept their input and take feedback into consideration. Their story is not your story, but their lessons learned may prevent you from repeating history, especially if it was a struggle.

Some students and their parents recommend colleges in name only. That is, they heard from their network about some great schools, and they believe in brand recognition. Everyone knows about the Ivy League and schools that have great football and basketball teams. They are great colleges, but are they great for you? Do they offer the major you desire, and do you meet the criteria to get in? Be comfortable with including these schools in your final list, but include them as an addition to those you selected through research and analysis. Remember, the entire philosophy of applying to college is that you should have *options* in the spring!

Attitude Is Everything

This is an important time in your life. You have a window of three to four months to lay the groundwork for the first phase of your adult life. It's important for you to communicate effectively with your parents and guidance counselor. This is a team approach, and it's all about you.

Your ability to manage the many steps and paperwork requirements is crucial. There are deadlines that you need to respect, and the stakes are high. Expect your parents to support you as well as question you about your progress. Use them as a resource and support system. Ask them questions and listen to the answers—they may affect your ultimate decisions. But remember, these are *your* choices and life plans.

Your guidance counselor is your expert advisor. Be comfortable asking for direction and assistance. You may have not spent quality time up until now, but this is crunch time. Your counselor's email address must be in your contacts, and you must keep him or her updated on your progress. Don't wait for your guidance counselor to contact you; reach out when you need to. Don't ignore your responsibilities; doing so will cause stress for both you and your team.

Final List

You are now at the point where you need to solidify your final list of colleges where you plan to apply. This list is a work in progress until the last final deadline arrives, so there is some wiggle room to add or remove schools. Create the perfect mix of schools based on additional Good Fit criteria, which may include commuting versus dorming, small versus large student body, moderate versus high cost, and so on.

Home or Away

You never know what the future holds. You may be dead set against attending a local college and living at home. But you should be prepared for some event or condition that makes you reconsider that option. Either way, you should have applications completed and acceptance pending from a *local* target school and reach school, so you have choices. These schools often participate in Immediate Decision Days, a special onsite registration program for students at your high school. Include them in your final list.

Size of School

Some students have concerns about being lost on a large campus among 15,000+ students, whereas others look forward to being part of a mini-city of large events and athletic competitions. There is no right or wrong answer other than personal preference. If you like to establish relationships with your professors, it is possible at both ends of the spectrum. It is merely based on your personal effort to seek out and connect with others. In addition, many large schools are mindful of developing a "school within a school." These programs foster a sense of community by academic program, dorm, or special interest.

> *I applied to about 12 colleges, with 4 being dream schools, 4 being backups, and the rest being suitable for me (based on academics). I was accepted to eight schools, rejected by four.*
>
> **—Mike H., Boston University, Massachusetts**

Point to Ponder

Large or small, you really won't know how you feel about a school until you walk around campus. Add schools to your list if you don't have the option to visit before applications are due, you can always travel in the spring.

When most people think of large schools, they think of students attending classes in huge lecture halls of 200+ students. This may or may not be true. No matter how large or small the student body, here are a few great questions to ask a campus representative, admissions rep, or tour guide: What is the largest class size? How many classes are in this format? Which courses? Even some small to medium-sized schools run introductory-level classes in a large, lecture-hall format, while other schools do not.

Tip

Some think schools report a student-to-faculty ratio in order to provide information about classes. However, it is not an accurate representation of class size; it is an indicator of how many professionals are on staff compared to the student body as a whole.

Campus Setting and Location

Some students have their hearts set on that perfect campus located in a small college town, while others dream of an urban experience. And others want the perfect combination of suburban life and amenities. Considering that the schools on your initial list are known for their academic strengths, include those that meet your personal preferences on the final list.

For those students choosing to live on campus, your parents may have thoughts or restrictions on how far you may travel. Don't let this bring you down. Figure out what's available and within reach. Sometimes a quick flight out of state to a college located near relatives seems more reasonable than a six-hour drive through the mountains.

Tip

Be mindful of working cooperatively with your parents. Their comfort level with your plans will have a direct impact on your relationship. Try to understand their concerns and address them accordingly.

Cost of Attendance

Right now, be open to including that very expensive college in your final list. When you receive your financial-aid package in the spring, you will discover how much of your award is in the form of student loans or gift aid. At that time, you can reconsider your financial or budgetary plan—how to pay for tuition, living expenses, and room and board. Either way, you want to have some lower-cost college options to choose from, so include those in your final list too.

For Athletes

Athletes need to accept this philosophy of having *options*, as well. You are being actively recruited by several schools because of your talents. However, it is advisable to apply to one or two other schools that will offer you admission based on a different factor, such as the merits of your transcript and honors. Again, you never know what the future will bring, and you always want to have options.

Compiling the Final List

Use Worksheet 12 to compile your final list of schools. Identify each school according to its Good Fit criteria:

- Safety school
- Target school
- Reach school
- Local safety school
- Local reach school
- Local—moderate cost
- Public college
- Private college
- Distance from home: short drive, long drive, airplane flight
- Campus setting: urban, suburban, rural
- Campus size: Small, medium, moderate, large, extra-large

Once completed, you will be ready to begin the application process.

Worksheet 12: Final List of Schools

College Name	Official Website Address	Good Fit Criteria

Chapter 9
Online Applications

Siena has a Facebook account, Twitter account, and other ways for students to follow our school. Our coordinator does a ton of trivia games and then sends prizes to prospective students who participated! It is a great way for students to get to know a school, as well as meet other classmates.

—**Lauren Mazurowski, Assistant Director of Admissions, Siena College, NY**

The research, planning and choices you have made up to now will make the rest of the application process much easier. You are focused; you have a purposeful list of schools and knowledge of the requirements. Now it's time to complete the actual college applications, but you have already accomplished a lot.

The majority of college applications are completed via the Internet. By accessing your secured account, you can begin to fulfill the requirements at your own pace. Upon completion, you can print out your materials for proofreading and recordkeeping purposes. Your data and documents will be transmitted to the school only upon the submission of your application and payment of the fee.

There is a slight chance that you may need to complete a paper application, but this is limited to special opportunities offered by local schools or to recruited athletes.

Access and Email

Since most, if not all, application procedures are conducted over the Internet, you must have a valid email address to have access to Internet portals and test-registration sites. Most students have had an email address for many years by this point, but they report that many of these accounts are overwhelmed by social-networking updates, advertisement emails, and spam. Because students are using email and the Internet more for social and information purposes, they don't always manage their accounts to easily notice important emails.

For Parents

Some parents prefer to use their own email accounts to register students for college entrance exams or application portals. This may not be an issue for your first child, but many websites, including www.collegeboard.com and www.fafsa.ed.gov, require unique email addresses for each applicant.

As previously recommended, each student should have an email account dedicated to the college application process. There are free email account opportunities at www.google.com, www.yahoo.com, and other sites. The account and password can be shared, and then both parents and students can monitor this email account for important information related to college research, test preparation and registration, applications, and financial aid. By creating and monitoring this dedicated account, you may also prevent a vital piece of information, such as the password to the supplemental application, being lost or overlooked.

Tip

Reminder: When you create or use an email account for the application process, please make sure your email address is appropriate and professional. It may not seem to matter when you're just using it to log in to a portal or register for an exam, but the admissions office staff member may notice it when he or she replies to one of your many questions. Keep it simple, such as using your first initial, last name, and lucky number to make it personalized and unique.

Public Education Systems

Many students seriously consider their own state and city's educational system for higher-education needs. Most of these well-established systems offer many varieties of programs, campuses, and level of competitiveness, all at a reasonable tuition when compared to private, nonprofit universities, which are self-funded. Don't forget that public universities receive partial funding from state and city budgets, a.k.a. tax revenue.

There is a catch: Because these public institutions receive funding from state and local government sources, reduced tuition is offered only to students who are legal residents of that particular state. Students from other states and municipalities are welcome to apply to and attend these public universities; however, they'll pay a higher rate of tuition, also known as non-resident tuition.

> **Note**
>
> Second Reminder: Each state determines its own residency requirements. Some states require students to be legal residents for one or two years prior to receiving the resident tuition rate. Others require students to graduate from a high school within the state. A few require students or their immediate families to own a residence in the state. Please refer your questions to the admissions office for specific residency requirements.

Not all public university systems are easily identified by their name, but some are. Here is a list of some of the largest, most popular state university systems and their web addresses:

State University of New York	SUNY	www.suny.edu/student
Pennsylvania State University	PSU	www.psu.edu
University of California	U Cal	www.universityofcalifornia.edu
California State University	Cal State	www.calstate.edu
City of New York	CUNY	www.cuny.edu

A benefit to using an Internet portal for your college applications is that you can apply to several campuses and programs using one form with all materials submitted simultaneously. In-state guidance counselors may have access to an administrative account or portal where they can easily upload school forms, transcripts, and supplemental materials.

> **For Parents**
>
> In the past, certain public colleges and universities have had marginal reputations for academic excellence and social experience. In recent years, there has been a new trend in the selectivity and competitiveness at most public institutions.
>
> Our economic conditions require all students to maximize the return on their investment with regard to college education, by choosing not to burden themselves with too much student debt by opting to attend the flagship or local college of their own state system. Because more and more qualified students are choosing this path, colleges are more selective about which students they admit, causing the average SAT/ACT scores to steadily increase.
>
> Students are now being waitlisted, deferred, and rejected from schools that previously had an open-enrollment policy a mere 10 years ago. Don't be surprised when you hear a sad tale from your student's peer about how he or she was rejected from a former "safety school."

The Application

Navigate to the official website and then familiarize yourself with the layout and navigation options of the homepage. See the hyperlinks along the left or right margin? Are there drop-down menu headings below the main title? Did you find small text links at the very bottom of the page?

Once you understand how the site is organized, you can look for what you need. There may be a link for Admissions, Freshman Admissions, Undergraduate Admissions, or even Prospective Students. Most colleges put a large Apply Here hyperlink on their main page; select it to begin!

The Apply Here link asks you to create an account with username and password. Don't forget to record your log-in information on Worksheet 4: Login/Password Organizer. You will be required to enter personal information about you and your parents; this is just the beginning. You may also need to refer to Worksheet 6: School Services Questionnaire to recall your high school's correct mailing address and CEEB code, as well as your guidance counselor's full name and contact information.

If you have your activity sheet, essays, and short answers completed, you can move swiftly through the application requirements. If you are completing items as you go, it may take a couple of weeks to get through the first application, but then the others will be a snap. When you have completed all of the required components for this school's application, you will be prompted to pay the application fee and submit.

Note

Please be aware that you may be required to mail certain documents. For example, if there is no link or form for you to upload your activity sheet or college essay, you must mail these items directly to the undergraduate admissions office.

Once the admissions office receives your documents, they will scan them into their system and attach them to your electronic application file. Make sure to include your full name (no nicknames) and address on each page.

Caution

After submitting your materials either electronically or by mail, it is imperative that you contact each and every school, either by phone or by email, to verify that they have received all required components to the application. Allow at least two weeks for processing, but you should do this before the stated deadline. Remember, just because you sent it or requested it to be sent, does not mean that it was received and properly filed.

Additional Materials

School-specific essays and questions are a great way for admissions officers to get more insight into an applicant and his or her plans. When you consider the college essay, it is usually two pages in length, can be about a wide variety of topics, and has been pored over, proofread, and edited at least 10 times.

The shorter school-specific essays and questions are usually more off the cuff—sometimes not edited, proofread, or even spell-checked. You may reveal some crucial information that may affect the admissions outcome in these non-threatening, simple responses.

> **Point to Ponder**
>
> Colleges and universities prefer to accept students who really want to attend their schools. The admissions office's main goal is to create, through acceptances, a full, balanced, freshman class of the highest-caliber students.

When you answer school-specific essays and questions, the admissions professionals may be able to determine the sincerity of your application. This could include how much you know about the school and its offerings, your opinion of the reputation or prestige of the school, and how well you weave your intended plans with the school's programs.

> **Tip**
>
> When you complete these supplemental materials, treat each school's application as if it is your first-choice school, because you want to gain acceptance to as many schools on your final list as possible. Remember, you created your list based on real factors of importance. In the spring, when the hard work is finished, you will choose from your acceptances according to final criteria of college visits, financial-aid packages, and other data.

Portfolios

Students interested in many creative/performance majors have an additional requirement to submit original works or auditions. Your creative arts teachers will guide you through the necessary items and format of your portfolio. These additional efforts support your admittance to a specific program and are often presented after you have submitted the college application. Your guidance counselor and college admissions staff can assist you in determining program-specific requirements and deadlines.

Performance/Sports Videos

If you have a special talent or are an athlete, it is important to share that information with colleges. You should first directly contact the head of the department, the coach, or the athletic director to inform them of your interest in their school. This introductory phone call or email should describe your talent and abilities while mentioning your contact information as well as your coach's, teacher's, or mentor's contact info.

Another high-tech option is to send your own performance video. By recording videos of you performing your talent in different settings, concerts, games, or tournaments, you bring your abilities and application to life. Using video-editing software available on your home computer or device, you can easily add music, titles, credits, and descriptive text or captions. Depending on the file size, you may email the file or just the link directly to coaches, professors, or the admissions staff.

Admissions Office

It is vitally important for you to connect with the admissions office staff. You can do this via email, college fairs, information presentations, information-request postcards, or website visits. Colleges track these communications, which to them represent your active interest in their school.

Depending on the size of the college and admissions staff, a staff member may be assigned to a specific state or area where he or she will actively represent and recruit for the college. Duties include networking with guidance counselors, hosting informational sessions at local high schools, and representing their school at local and national college fairs.

> **Point to Ponder**
>
> Some of these staff members participate in the decision-making process; they may review application materials, be the sole decision-maker, and/or work with the committee to determine admission decisions. Either way, these are important people to network with during the college application process.

Facebook is not a new thing, and I would recommend that a student not "like" or "friend" any admissions professionals until they are accepted. Facebook is a way for the student to show interest, but not all types of students should use Facebook. If a student is going to post pictures of himself doing keg stands, etc., I would recommend to them not to "friend" any college/university staff. The benefit of Facebook is that you are able to get questions answered within minutes and maintain better contact with admissions staffers.

—Emmanuel Cruz, Admissions Counselor, Hartwick College, New York

The Common App

The Common Application website and portal is a universal or standard application where you can apply to many schools and programs at once. It is similar to the public education portals in terms of its convenience and streamlined approach. However, the member colleges and universities that participate in the www.commonapp.org website are not limited by location or type.

There are no disadvantages to using the Common Application. It is a wonderful time-saving tool that enables you to apply to many member colleges and universities using the same interface. You can view a listing of schools who accept the Common App by visiting their official website at https://www.commonapp.org/CommonApp/Members.aspx.

After you navigate to the homepage, you must locate the Create an Account link. When you're logged in, add schools to your My Colleges personal portfolio. As you navigate and enter the required data, save after each page and return as necessary. Again, be prepared to complete each application over the course of a few days or weeks.

The Common Application portal allows you to upload your completed college essay in its final version under the Writing tab. There is also the opportunity to upload additional information or a document, which could be used for your completed activity sheet.

For added convenience, there is the option for you to invite school officials to write recommendations on your behalf via email generated by the Common App. The term "officials" sounds serious, but it really refers to your guidance counselor, teachers, or other recommenders. It's a great opportunity to save an envelope and stamp.

For now, the opportunity to Invite Officials is located under the School Forms tab; the link will appear only after you have completed the FERPA (privacy) waiver.

Exciting news: Next year, the Common Application will be unveiling a newly redesigned web portal for your application needs.

Second reminder: To request a letter of recommendation, you must politely ask your teacher or coach to write you a letter of recommendation and provide him or her with supporting details, including a draft or completed version of your activity sheet. Ideally, professionals write well-crafted, detailed, high-energy letters describing your achievements, effort, and qualities.

If you invite them using the Common Application feature, you need to enter their full name and email address. Invited "officials" receive an email alert informing them of your request. The teachers, using their own IDs and passwords, log in, complete a brief checklist, and upload the letter directly to the site.

> **Tip**
>
> The Common Application also gives guidance counselors an administrative portal to use to facilitate the application process for their students. Counselors can view application materials and submission statuses.

Because the Common Application is a universal application form, the website provides the opportunity for colleges and universities to add their own supplemental requirements to the site. You may need to follow the appropriate links to view and complete the required elements, which may include school-specific essays and/or short-response questions.

> **Tip**
>
> Complete all essays and short-response questions in your preferred word processing software that includes a spell-check feature, word count, and printing functions. This also allows you to easily proofread and save the file for future use or referral. Copy and paste your work to the appropriate form when ready.

When you finish each school's required components, print the final version of your Common Application and then ask a parent or trusted adult to review all of the data and give a final proofread. When you are satisfied with your work, pay the required fee and submit the application and supplements using three separate processes. Second reminder: Fees are typically paid via credit card using the secured payment site.

> **For Parents**
>
> It is important for you to review your student's applications. You are a valued stakeholder in this process. Not only are you providing emotional and financial support, but you must be the extra set of eyes that can identify errors and omissions. These errors and omissions may be cause for waitlisting, deferral, or worse, rejection or loss of financial aid. Even if you didn't go to college or complete applications using the Internet, your level of patience and general understanding of organizations and attention to details will allow you to be your student's greatest advocate.

Individual Schools

Many schools are neither part of a public education system nor a member of the Common Application; however, don't be alarmed or discouraged from applying. The process is exactly the same; you just need to complete the requirements using their website.

Second reminder: Most college and university websites end with the extension .edu. Knowing this will assist you in locating the official website. Every school designs their website according to their own needs, target audience, and plan. When researching admissions criteria, majors offered, and school statistics, you will find information in different locations, but be confident that it is there somewhere.

Immediate Decision Days

Immediate Decision Days are a great opportunity for students who plan to study locally during their college education. At most high schools, local public and private colleges and universities plan a special day to offer onsite registration to qualified students.

Traditionally, the guidance department posts a listing of program participants at least one month before their scheduled date. This listing may include minimum GPA and SAT/ACT requirements for intended applicants.

If you meet the minimum standards and are interested in applying to one or more schools on the list, you must sign up for an appointment. In preparation for your meeting, you may need to compile the required documents. This normally includes a completed paper application or print out, an official or unofficial transcript, an activity sheet, letters of recommendation, a college essay, test scores, and any other supplemental materials.

You should use a folder to organize documents for each school for which you plan to attend an onsite registration appointment. Provide a copy of the requirements for each folder/school. The admissions representative that you meet with will keep these documents to establish your admission file at his or her office.

Bring your folder and materials with you to the appointment. This meeting is part interview, part records review. The admissions representative may ask you brief questions about your interests, intended major, and extracurricular activities. He or she will read your application documents to provide you with an immediate admissions decision, especially if you meet or exceed the stated requirements.

If your GPA and/or SAT/ACT scores are slightly below the stated requirements, the admissions representative may not determine an immediate decision but may offer to bring your application back to the office for committee review. This is not terrible news; it just means that another admissions professional must provide feedback and input to support the decision.

There are great advantages to participating in Immediate Decision Days: You can receive an acceptance immediately upon submitting your applications, early in the process. This could take a lot of stress off of you and your parents, knowing that you already have been accepted to college. Often, colleges waive the application fee, so you can save money by taking advantage of this in-school event. Finally, admissions representatives may have the authority to offer scholarships on the spot based on GPA and admissions-test scores.

Students often leave onsite registration appointments with a sense of excitement, achievement, and relief.

Note

Even though you receive acceptances early in the fall, you still have until the common May 1st deadline to make your decision.

Tip

Many students use this program to gain acceptance to local schools considered safety and target options. Even though these schools are local, there still may be the option of living on campus.

For Parents

It's important to keep in mind that your student is making decisions based on information that he or she currently has available. It's unfortunate, but there is always the chance that as your student learns more about a major or even a school, he or she may be inclined to have a change of heart. Be realistic. Expect ideas and plans to change during this time. If you dare, remember what you planned as a teenager. Ask yourself whether it all worked out the way you thought? Anticipate your student's stressful breakdown or panic attack. Breathe.

U.S. Military Academies

Some students are looking to the federal government's service academies for their outstanding training, education, and job-placement reputation, where they receive a free education in exchange for military service. Due to the additional and somewhat extensive application requirements, interested applicants and their families must begin preparing early on in high school, while gaining the assistance of guidance counselors and recruitment specialists.

Cadets accepted to these institutions are expected to be student leaders of good moral character who possess outstanding academic records. They must pass a physical fitness test and medical examination and obtain a congressional nomination.

- United States Air Force Academy at www.usafa.af.mil or www.academyadmissions.com
- United States Coast Guard Academy[1] at www.cga.edu
- United States Merchant Marine Academy at www.usmma.edu
- United States Military Academy (West Point) at www.usma.edu
- United States Naval Academy at www.usna.edu

---

[1] Applicants to the U.S. Coast Guard Academy do not require congressional nomination.

Interested students should visit the academy's official website to complete an online pre-candidate questionnaire by the end of junior year. However, a commitment to academic success and community-service activism must be made well before then.

Once admission staff conduct a pre-screening assessment of your candidacy, upon approval you will receive a packet detailing specific application instructions, requirements, and deadlines.

Early Decision versus Early Action—Big Difference

This is a totally optional but critical part of the application process; it can be very serious if the programs are confused, as both require you to submit your materials early.

Early decision (*ED*) is considered a once-in-a-lifetime commitment, especially because it is legally binding. By applying ED to one school, you agree to attend it if you're accepted, while rescinding or revoking your applications at all other schools.

This all has to be done without knowledge of the possible financial-aid package being offered. Not many students choose this method of application. Some experts say that it improves your chances for acceptance, but that has not been proven.

Traditionally, the early-decision deadline is November 1st, but some schools offer two. Please check with the college's official website or admissions office for this information. If you are accepted ED, there are perks that include preferred residence-hall choices and knowing that your fate is decided well before most of your classmates. Congratulations!

If you're not accepted ED, some schools will consider your application again with the pool of regular-decision applicants; sadly others will consider your admission decision final. Either way, you are then free to apply to other schools and consider their acceptances until the May 1st universal deadline.

Early action (*EA*) is more of a priority/fast-track experience. When you submit your application materials early, possibly by an October 15th or November 15th deadline, you are on target to receive an admission decision earlier than other applicants. There is no contractual agreement or requirement to attend and you may have the opportunity to apply EA to more than one school.

Restrictive early action is a relatively new program, gaining in popularity, where a college prevents you from participating in other schools' EA processes at the same time as theirs. It allows students to identify their first-choice school by expressing extreme interest without the pressures of a legally binding commitment.

Schools have the option to set their own admission programs and deadlines. Please check with the college's official website or admissions office for this information. Your guidance counselor is a great resource to tap when deciding to take advantage of either of these options. Keep him or her updated about your plans and goals with open lines of communication either in person or through email.

Regular Decision versus Rolling Decision

The choice between regular decision and rolling decision is not yours to make. These terms describe the method in which the college reviews applications and notifies students. It doesn't even impact how you apply, for all intents and purposes.

Regular decision requires all applications to be due by a specific date—say, January 1st. At that time, all files will be reviewed by the admissions staff, and applicants are notified of the admissions decisions on a particular date—say, March 1st. Accepted students have until the universal May 1st deadline to make a final decision.

Rolling decision describes a process in which applications are received daily during the fall months, and applicants are notified of admission decisions in a timely matter, usually six to eight weeks after receipt. Accepted students still have until the universal deadline of May 1st to make their final decision.

Some professionals recommend applying early to colleges that use rolling admissions, which may allow applicants to have a better chance of acceptance. If you can submit your documents early, do it, but don't rush to submit unfinished, incomplete, or unproofed documents. That can hurt your chances more than help them.

Application-Tracking

It is your responsibility to inform your guidance counselor of the colleges where you apply. This is commonly done using a form that provides the counselor with the details he or she needs to successfully submit school forms necessary to complete your application. If your school subscribes to Naviance, your entries and list of schools you are applying to will indicate your plans to your guidance counselor, so a separate form may not be necessary.

Just so you know: A counselor sends your high school profile, which details the grading structure and course framework of your school; the counselor's letter of recommendation, which details your growth, special circumstances, and special interests throughout your high school career; any additional supporting materials; and your official transcript. It is vital for your counselor to know if you plan to apply ED or EA because there are strict deadlines that need to be met by him or her also.

> **Caution**
>
> The plan to apply early decision, which is legally binding, should be made in conjunction with the counseling department, who has the insight and experience to guide individual students while explaining strategies and concerns.

Your counselor may provide you with a form similar to the sample in Reference Sheet E to track your plans and applications. It is important for you to submit this information to your counselor as soon as possible. There will be opportunities for you to edit or add additional colleges during the process.

Reference Sheet E: Sample Form: Application-Tracking Sheet

Student Name: Date Submitted:

Guidance Counselor:

College Name	Via Common App.org?	ED or EA	Application Due Date	Intended Major	Guidance Materials Submitted Date/Initials	By Internet or Mail

It is just as important for you to keep excellent records of your application submissions and deadlines. Since it is not possible or advisable to complete an entire application in one sitting, there will be times when you need to stop, save your work, and return to the application in a day or two, after you get the information you need or have more time to devote to it.

Because you're going to be completing applications at various times, either in order of importance or early admission/early decision due dates, it's important for you to keep track of your progress. Even if you choose to use www.commonapp.org for all of your application needs, there are different supplemental requirements for each school, and you'll submit each independently.

Use Worksheet 13: Your In-Progress Tracking Sheet to track your progress for each of your college applications. It is especially helpful when you're completing requirements online and you don't have paper documents to account for. Circle options, check off requirements, and add dates where listed.

> *I was surprised that my daughter was waitlisted at one school, and it wasn't one of her reach schools. We knew something went wrong, especially since she was accepted by other schools that were much more competitive. When we looked closer, we realized that her application wasn't complete as of the deadline for her early action application.*
>
> **—Ronnie B., parent of high school senior**

Use Worksheet 14: Contact Info for Admissions Offices to create a handy reference sheet for you and your parents to use when contacting admissions staff.

Worksheet 13:
Your In-Progress Tracking Sheet

College Name: _____

Web Address: _____

User Name: _____

Password Hint: _____

Circle: Early Decision   Early Action   Regular Decision

       Rolling Admissions   Deadline Date: _____

Basic Personal Information

Entered and Completed: ☐   Date:_____

Additional Information Needed

SAT Scores Sent: ☐   Date:_____

ACT Scores Sent: ☐   Date:_____

SAT Subject Test Scores Sent (if required): ☐ Date:_____

Requested Letters of Recommendation

Teacher #1: _____   Online   Stamped, Addressed Envelope
Date: _____

Teacher #2: _____   Online   Stamped, Addressed Envelope
Date: _____

Other #3: _____   Online   Stamped, Addressed Envelope
Date: _____

Supplemental Forms

Activity Sheet Completed: ☐   Attached/Uploaded   Mailed

Date: _____

College Essay Completed: ☐   Attached/Uploaded   Mailed

Date: _____

Additional Essays Completed: ☐ Attached/Uploaded   Mailed

Date: _____

Paid Application Fee: ☐

Date: _____

Common Application and Supplementals Submitted: ☐

Date: _____

Special Circumstances

Coaches Contacted (if required): ☐   Date:_____

Audition Scheduled (if required): ☐   Date:_____

Interview Scheduled (if required): ☐   Date:_____

Sent Transcript Request to Guidance: ☐   Date:_____

Completed CSS/Profile Financial Aid (if required): ☐ Date:_____

Contacted Admissions to Verify ALL Application Materials Received**

Via Email: ☐   Phone: ☐   Date:_____

Notes:

** As the deadline for each application approaches, it is your responsibility to contact the admissions office of each college to *verify* that your materials have been received and that your application is complete and ready for review.

Worksheet 14:
Contact Info for Admissions Offices

College Name	Admissions Office Phone Number Contact Name	Contact Email Address	Application Complete? (Notes)

Now, knowing the potential input that this admissions professional has in your college future, what efforts are you going to put forth to establish a relationship? Any ideas?

Here's the plan: When a college comes to your school for an informational presentation, even if you know everything about that school, sign up anyway. Ask informative questions, participate, and introduce yourself at the end if the opportunity is available. If possible, mention that this school is one of your top-choice schools. And get the admissions professional's contact information, including phone number and email address.

The admissions representative will add your contact information to a database of prospective students. Every time you contact the college in any manner, it will be recorded in the database. This record of effort or contact can be thought of as extreme interest in the school. Second reminder: Admissions officers want to accept students who really want to attend their school. No one wants to be rejected—you or the school.

When you go to a college fair, look to see whether that same admissions rep is working the table for the college. Check in. Fill out a request-for-information card again, if possible, and leave it. This will count as more "interest" in the database.

When you visit the college, make sure that you go to the admissions office to sign in and schedule a tour. Even if you've been to the campus 10 times because your best friend's sister went there, it's important that the admissions staff knows that you took the time, effort, and resources to visit their school. Again, this is showing sincere interest in attending.

Finally, if you have any questions—and even if you don't—begin an appropriate email correspondence with the admissions rep. Ask for additional information or clarification. Ask about extracurricular opportunities, club sports, or travel information.

The number of email correspondences will be added to the database, and the content of each email will be included with your application materials in your electronic file. So, it's important that you are professional and well-spoken/written when you are writing these emails.

Don't send questionable pictures. We don't need a student's junior prom photo, senior portraits, summer vacation pics, family portraits, etc. or prayer cards, world-vision pledge cards, and free Bibles. (People actually send these things with their file.) You can't send gifts in exchange for acceptance, and this also includes subscriptions to magazines, etc.

—Emmanuel Cruz, Admissions Counselor, Hartwick College, New York

---

PART V
Costs and Cash

Nowadays most students applying to college report feeling stressed by the financial expectations of higher education as compared to college admissions requirements and anticipated workload. With rising tuition costs and limited resources, many are relying on large amounts of student-loan debt to get the job done.

It doesn't have to be that way for you or any other student. There are plenty of options available to you, allowing you to earn a degree while living within a sensible budget that is mindful of present and future finances. Now that your applications are in process or already submitted, we can look at some of the finer details of paying for college.

Chapter 10
Tuition and More

*College visits are **very** important! Visit for a tour, an information session, a large program, or an interview. Anything! It plays a big part in committee review. I would also say to visit once during the search process and another time when you are down to the final choices. That shows consistent interest in a school.*

*—**Lauren Mazurowski, Assistant Director of Admissions, Siena College, New York***

To keep it real, recognize that your budget and financial situation carry a lot of weight in your final decision. Accordingly, you must calculate and analyze carefully so you make this decision based on accurate data.

Total Cost of Attendance

Total cost of attendance represents the entire amount of funds needed to attend college and pay all necessary expenses each year. These expenditures are not limited to tuition and your dorm room and meal plan, also known as *room and board*. Often print and web resources will list these amounts, but there are many other costs associated with attending college.

Depending on your situation, you can fund your college experience with money from different sources, which include your savings, money from parents and relatives, work, student loans, scholarships, grants, and so on. It's important to consider how you will pay for the following categories of expenses:

- **Tuition.** This is the fee to attend classes, and it is paid prior to the start of each semester. Costs stated on the college's official website are the most accurate and up to date, but beware: You may experience increases during your enrollment. Also, expect to be charged minor additional fees for computer, health services, and fitness facilities.

- **Room and board.** These fees are paid prior to the start of each semester. Most freshmen are required to live in on-campus housing. Room styles and meal plans options vary. Choices and costs stated on the college's official website are the most accurate and up to date.

- **Housing.** After freshman year, many students choose to live in private housing near campus. Students live together and share common expenses—rent and utilities. Costs vary depending on campus setting, size of house/apartment, and number of students sharing the space. Cleaning and maintenance expenditures are divided among renters. Roommates are responsible for their own food costs, and some still opt to purchase a meal plan for the convenience of eating on campus. Often, total costs are lower than standard on-campus room-and-board rates.

- **Commuting expenses.** Gasoline, car/lease payments, and insurance are major costs for students who choose to commute to school rather than live on campus. You can calculate these weekly and monthly costs using estimates and distance traveled.

- **Books and school supplies.** The costs for textbooks, notebooks, and assorted supplies vary depending on your course load for the semester; you purchase these items prior to the beginning of classes. Opportunities to buy e-books, used books, and discount supplies are available. Costs for these items can average $500 per semester.

- **Transportation.** The total of these expenses depends on the campus setting and location; costs vary. Most schools don't allow freshmen to have cars on campus, so expenses are limited to bus/taxi fare and travel back and forth from campus to home, as necessary.

- **Auto.** After freshman year, many students hope to bring their cars to college, which allows them to get to work, shopping, social events, and home at their convenience. If there are no costs attributable to the car, then include insurance and maintenance costs in your estimate.

- **Gasoline/Tolls.** Depending on the price of gas and distance traveled, gasoline and toll costs will vary.

- **Cell phone.** This necessary equipment is usually bundled with a family plan. Students require access to technology, which includes text messaging, email, and Internet capabilities.

- **Computer.** Students rely heavily on technology, both for entertainment and for school use. College campuses have ample labs, and students have almost constant access to facilities. However, students benefit from owning a personal computer, and most choose laptop computers over desktop models. Assignments are often completed and submitted via the Internet, so some students carry laptops and tablet-style computers to class to access online notes and handouts. Major retailers offer student discounts on equipment and software, so check with the store sales team or your school's admissions office for details.

- **Toiletries and household items.** These are required items for all, but students living away at school should include personal toiletries, cleaning supplies, paper goods, and other products in their budget.

Most schools employ emergency-notification systems, which allows school administration to alert students via text or email in the event of an emergency on or around campus.

- **Entertainment.** Each campus and surrounding area offers its own specific opportunities for entertainment, which depend on the location, geography, and culture of the community. Activities include many low- or no-cost options for students, such as on-campus movies, shows, and events. However, some schools, especially those set in urban settings, require students to have a sufficient amount of pocket money for entertainment purposes.

- **Food and drink.** Even with a substantial meal plan, students want and need to purchase food and drink from the outside world. Some students split pizzas to enhance the fun and effectiveness of late-night studying or homework sessions, while others may want to enjoy lunch or dessert in town with friends.

For some students, parents and student savings will assist in paying for most of these costs, but no matter what, someone has to pay. Even if your parents continue paying phone and car expenses, it is very important to be aware of how much money they spend on your behalf.

Additionally, students funding their own college experience with savings, loans, and scholarships/grants need to have a realistic and accurate picture of how much money is needed for their college education, when either commuting or living on campus.

Complete Worksheet 15: Personalized Total Cost of Attendance to determine an estimate of the annual total expenditures. Use a separate worksheet for each college you are considering.

Note

Worksheet 15 includes costs that recur each year. It does not include items that you may need to purchase to furnish your dorm room or live away from home. These additional costs will be discussed in Chapter 14, "Topics to Anticipate."

For Parents

To teach your student to budget his or her funds each semester, you can agree upon a set dollar amount for personal, entertainment, and food/snack expenditures. These costs are very readily and easily controlled. Your student has the option to use income earned from part-time and summer jobs, if available, to supplement these funds.

PRINT THIS!

Worksheet 15: Personalized Total Cost of Attendance

Based on Annual Amounts

College Name:	(Annually = Fall & Spring Semesters)
Tuition	$
Housing:	$
Room (Residence Hall)	$
Board (Meal Plan)	$
Off Campus Housing (Rent & Utilities)	$
Living at Home	$
Books (may vary, but average $500/semester)	$
Transportation:	$
Travel	$
Auto	$
Gasoline/Tolls	$
Insurance	$
Maintenance	$
Computer Equipment/Cell Phone	$
Toiletries/Household/Laundry	$
Health Insurance/Medical	$
Personal Care:	$
Hair/Nails	$
Clothing	$
Entertainment	$
Food/Snacks	$
Other	$
Other	$
Other	$
TOTAL ANNUAL COST OF ATTENDING COLLEGE	$

Note

New laws designed to protect college students from credit-card debt require parental consent for students under age 21. You and your family will determine whether a credit card, either in your or your parent's name, is necessary and guidelines for its use—for emergency purposes only or other agreed-upon expenses.

The current generation prefers to make purchases using ATM and debit cards. It is important for you to understand the rules and fees associated with these cards. Speak with your banking representative for more details.

Tip

You should research the option to open a basic or student bank account at a bank close to or actually on campus. This local convenience may reduce fees for out-of-network ATM and banking transactions. Ask an admissions office staff member for a listing of local banks.

Net Price Calculator

The Net Price Calculator is a web-based tool used to estimate how much and what types of financial aid you will qualify for when attending college. As of October 1, 2011, federal law requires all colleges and universities to have the Net Price Calculator feature on their websites. To meet this requirement, some schools link to an external third-party website, such as www.collegeboard.org, which completes the calculations to estimate the cost of attendance and expected financial-aid package for students and their families.

Caution

The Net Price Calculator is another tool used to provide information to assist you with college selection and budgetary planning. Results are an estimate based on information you enter. Amounts are only as accurate as the personal and financial data you provide.

When it is time for you to make your final decision about school, use only bona fide sources of financial information, which are the financial-aid award letters that you will receive in late winter/early spring, and your analysis on Worksheet 15: Personalized Total Cost of Attendance.

Point to Ponder

To locate the Net Price Calculator, navigate to the school's official website. Locate the search box, traditionally in the top-right corner of the homepage. Type the phrase "Net Price Calculator" and press Enter. Hyperlinks to the appropriate page will appear at the top of the results listing.

You may first be directed to a page that lists tuition and cost descriptions, how the calculator works, and additional fees and terms. Be aware that you may still need to click another hyperlink to arrive at the Net Price Calculator tool to begin the process. Reminder: Hyperlinks usually appear as blue, underlined text.

Use Worksheet 16 to organize and record figures needed to complete the Net Price Calculator. By first documenting information on this sheet, you can complete the process for many schools easily and consistently.

Your Cash

It is important for you to have a true understanding of your financial situation. Many parents do not feel comfortable speaking with their children about such serious topics. Often, they don't know how to even start this conversation, while students don't know which questions to ask. Use the interview-style Worksheet 17: Assess Your Financial Situation to get a basic awareness of how you stand financially.

Overall, the college application process for me was not that stressful. In the beginning, before I knew what exactly everything was about, I did stress a little bit. Honestly, if it wasn't for Ms. Portnoy, I don't think the process would have been as smooth. Thanks to her, my organization throughout the whole process was good. The hardest part for me was deciding which colleges I liked and was able to apply to. After determining that I already had my essay, activity sheet, etc., the whole application process was not that hard. My parents helped me a lot, not only paying for the applications, but also taking me to schools and helping me weigh out my options. My guidance counselor was always there to answer my questions, usually through email. Altogether, I am glad that my application process is done, and now the most stressful part is waiting to see if I've been accepted.

—**Danielle G., high school senior**

Worksheet 16: Data Needed to Complete Net Price Calculator

Student Information:

Name

Year of Birth

State of Legal Residence

Marital Status

Dependents

Campus Housing

Citizenship

Merit Scholar?

Parent Information:

Marital Status

Year of Birth

State of Legal Residence

Siblings/Names/Ages

Tax Form Filed in Previous Year

Parent Income from Last Year's Tax Return/Forms:

Wages

Interest and Dividends

Business Income/Losses

Adjustments to Income

Education Tax Credits

Non-Taxable Retirement Account Contributions

Child Support Received

Itemized Deductions

Exemptions Claimed

Parent Finances:

Cash/Savings/Checking (Parents)

Own/Rent?

Value/Mortgage/Purchase Price/Year of Purchase/
Rental Amount

Value of Investments (Parents)

Business Owner?

Farm Owner?

Other Real Estate Owned

Estimated Medical Expenses Not Covered by Insurance

Elementary, Secondary Tuition Paid for Siblings

Student Finances:

Earnings from Work

Interest and Dividend Income

Untaxed Income and Benefits

Cash/Savings/Checking/Investments

Owns a Home?

Owns a Business/Farm?

Equity in Real Estate Owned

Value of Trusts

After you enter the required information, the tool will calculate your Estimated Total Cost of Attendance, Estimated Grant/Gift Aid, Estimated Net Price, and Estimated Self Help (from loans and work), revealing the amount of Estimated Remaining Costs.

The next step brings you to a Resource Sheet where you can make a plan to address the Estimated Remaining Costs, which must be funded from resources other than those listed above.

Resources include:

Parent Contribution from Income

Student Contribution from Income

Student Summer Savings

Parent Contribution from Savings

Gift from Family and Friends

529 College Savings Plans

Outside Scholarships

Outside Grants

Worksheet 17:
Assess Your Financial Situation

1. How much money do you have in savings to put toward your college education—undergraduate only?

2. How much money can your parents contribute each year while you are in college?

3. Will anyone else help pay for your college-related expenses? If so, how much can you expect?

4. Do you plan to live at home or away at college?

5. Do you expect to receive a sports or academic scholarship? If so, for what amount?

6. Will you work part-time or full-time while school is in session?

7. Will you work part-time or full-time while classes are *not* in session? (For example, summer and winter breaks.) How much will you make? If so, will this money go toward tuition and room and board *or* your personal expenses?

8. List, by name only, expenditures that *you* must pay while in college. For example, books, cell phone, car payment, insurance, gas, food, clothing, entertainment, and personal and office supplies.

9. Must you attend graduate school to gain employment in your chosen career field?

10. Are you counting on financial aid in the form of student loans to help finance your college expenses? If so, how much debt are you willing to take on to pay for your undergraduate degree? How does this amount compare to the annual salary you expect to earn when you enter your career field?

Budgeting

Now that you have assessed both sides of the equation, your expenses and financial support, with the assistance of your team of family and guidance counselor, you are ready to evaluate the results.

To make your final analysis more straightforward and even a little easier, contemplate answers to these questions while you wait to receive admissions decisions:

- Overall, how does the total cost of attendance for each school compare to your financial situation?

- Which schools on your final list create the *most* long-term financial responsibility/stress for you and your family?

- Which schools create the *least* long-term financial responsibility/stress for you and your family?

- Which schools agree with your vision of going to college and don't break the bank for you and your family?

So get involved, party, and have fun—just not too much because then you can't wake up, and you will end up missing your morning class. Study—it's not a joke. If you don't study, you'll fail. Pay attention in class, do your homework, don't be too clicked in to your roommate, because spending too much time with one person is not good.

—Steve C., York College of Pennsylvania

You will get lost around your campus the first few weeks, but then after a couple of weeks, you should be fine.

—Jessica F., Seton Hall University, New Jersey

Chapter 11
Financial Aid

The college process has been a nightmare, to be honest. I personally feel I visited **way** *too many colleges. After all of the places I visited, they all kind of blur together. I still have to finish my SUNY apps; I just forgot I had to do them. I gave up on my application to one school because it is currently $60,000 a year, so there is no way I could afford to go there. My new number-one school is in Pennsylvania. I got my acceptance letter yesterday along with a $14,000 scholarship to go there, and I've visited twice. I really love the school, and I can't wait to visit again. My mom said I have to write them a letter to ask for more money because the cost is really high, but asking a school for money seems really awkward. I hope they do give me more money, though.*

—Faith Y., high school senior

Paying for college is a big responsibility, so you must seriously devise a plan to pay for tuition and expenses. Most students look to and count on the various forms of financial aid to foot the bill, along with some help from parents.

You need to be knowledgeable about the different types of financial aid available to you and your family. It can be a confusing topic, overwhelming to both students and parents. Although the financial-aid application process is straightforward, it is also in-depth and deadline-oriented.

The financial-aid analysis and offer you receive from each school may be one of your greatest determining factors when deciding which school to attend. If you complete your forms accurately and take advantage of the best available opportunities, financial aid will not be the *only* deciding factor.

Grants and Scholarships

Scholarships and grants are financial-aid monies for college that do not have to be repaid. They are considered *gift aid* and should be the focus of your efforts.

Government and college scholarships and grants are based on either merit or need. *Merit awards* are offered by admissions officers to entice higher-achieving students who have GPAs and test scores above the average range for that particular school. They can also be awarded to students pursuing specific majors or representing an underserved population, career field, or demographic.

Need-based aid, in the form of grants, is awarded depending on your and your parents' personal and financial data, as submitted on the Free Application for Federal Student Aid (FAFSA). Many factors are considered when determining aid, so even "wealthy" families are advised to complete this form annually.

The U.S. Department of Education offers many grants, including:

- Federal Pell grants
- Federal Supplemental Educational Opportunity grants (FSEOG)
- Teacher Education Assistance for College and Higher Education (TEACH) grants
- Iraq and Afghanistan Service grants

The official Federal Student Aid website at www.studentaid.ed.gov lists program requirements and details to assist both students and families in navigating the financial-aid process.

Your preferred Internet search engine can assist you in locating the Grants and Scholarships page from the Office of Higher Education on your state's official government website, which you can use to identify additional grant and scholarship opportunities. Please note that all official U.S. government websites have the extension .gov in their IP or web address.

> **Warning**
>
> You should never be charged a fee to access scholarship and grant information or to apply for financial aid. It is the *Free* Application for Federal Student Aid (FAFSA). The Internet is full of legitimate, helpful information, but there are also potential scams and dangers. Contact your guidance counselor for assistance.

The largest source of gift aid comes from national and local corporations and organizations that want to give back to support their communities by offering outside grants and scholarships worth millions of dollars. There are limitless opportunities in this category of gift aid; it just takes a little work. Many times it's not necessary for applicants to prove financial need as a requirement to win these scholarships, so these monies are available to everyone.

Local Opportunities

Scholarships offered by civic organizations, corporations, and local nonprofits and in memoriam of students and staff require an application, which may include an essay, a high GPA, community service experience, and/or involvement in certain activities or groups.

Those who devote resources, such as time and money, to fund these scholarships really want to see the awards go to worthy students. They consider it their way to "pay it forward" to future generations. Please take advantage of these opportunities whenever and wherever they present themselves.

Review Worksheet 6: School Services Questionnaire to determine where your guidance office maintains an updated listing of scholarship opportunities available to local students—usually either posted in their office or on their website or through links on the Naviance portal. Check back frequently, as new scholarship opportunities are added throughout the year.

You must adhere to very specific requirements, guidelines, and deadlines when you're applying, with some scholarships requiring "demonstrated financial need" as determined by scholarship administrators. Apply for all local scholarships, because your chances of winning are significantly higher when you're competing solely against neighboring students! There may be no limit to the total amount of money awarded!

> **For Parents**
>
> This is a crucial time for you to assist and motivate your student. It is too easy for students to rely on loans as their primary source of financial aid when all they have to do is "sign on the dotted line," and their needs are met. Some students are surprised to find that they must pay $600 per month in student-loan payments starting within six months of graduation.
>
> Help students to perceive reality—a fast-forward to age 24, when they are starting their careers, living in their first apartments, and paying bills plus making student-loan payments. Emphasize that any and all money received through scholarships and grants will be less money repaid with interest in the future.

Don't forget to ask your parents to check with the Human Resources departments at their jobs for available scholarship opportunities. Often companies award gift aid to deserving children of their dedicated employees. Similarly, banks and credit unions offer scholarships to children of their member-customers. Ask them all! Businesses love the goodwill that comes from supporting community members, especially students in pursuit of their dreams.

Scholarship Databases

National scholarship databases are the most effective way to identify scholarship opportunities. FastWeb and Sallie Mae both offer free scholarship search tools at www.fastweb.com and http://go.salliemae.com/scholarship/default.aspx, respectively. The list of scholarships is overwhelming, but if you create an accurate profile, the search engine will deliver opportunities geared to you.

After navigating to the website, create an account that will store your profile and scholarship opportunities. Don't forget to record your user name and password hint on Worksheet 4: Login/Password Organizer.

You will be asked many questions pertaining to your interests, activities, affiliations, religion, heritage, and career aspirations. There will also be questions about your parents' backgrounds, degrees of education, and career fields. These questions aren't meant to be nosy or intrusive; rather, they are specifically designed to determine whether you meet the requirements of certain scholarships. Don't skip this section or enter inaccurate information—it will affect your results and may cause you to miss a great opportunity.

After you submit your profile, the site searches through the database to find all relevant opportunities and then lists the results. With the assistance of a helpful family member or two, you must read the scholarship summaries and requirements to determine which are worthwhile efforts, saving potential opportunities as "Favorites" for future reference.

> **For Parents**
>
> The scholarship listing, overwhelming to students, offers hundreds of entries with lots of fine print. This is your time to shine! If you can identify the best scholarships for your student, to let him or her focus exclusively on meeting the requirements to apply, it is time well spent! Also, being mindful of deadlines and providing postal supplies is always appreciated.

> **Note**
>
> FastWeb, Sallie Mae, and other scholarship search engines do not distribute any scholarship money themselves. They offer a searchable database of titles and summaries to earn income through advertising and referrals. So watch out for screens that appear in between steps that advertise specific schools or services. They are not part of your scholarship results, but they are a necessity when operating a business on the Internet. Look for the "No Thanks" link in small print at the bottom of these pages!

When you're ready to begin the scholarship application process, return to those "Favorites" and follow the links to proceed to the website of the organization, business, or person who administers and awards the scholarships. Here you will find the official submission requirements, methods, and deadlines. Make sure to adhere to guidelines and submit all requirements by the deadline, so you don't get disqualified.

> **Tip**
>
> According to student feedback, scholarship-search websites take their job of notifying you of potential scholarships and opportunities very seriously. Some students are annoyed by the number of email notices they receive. Please adjust settings to meet your preferences.

Real Opportunities

Apply for as many scholarships as possible! It is important to start this process early: Begin it by the end of your junior year and continue it throughout the summer. During fall of your senior year, you will be too busy preparing for the SATs/ACTs and submitting college applications, so you can pick up where you left off after your applications have been submitted and keep going until you have exhausted all opportunities!

It is a wonderful feeling to meet the requirements of a scholarship application with materials you've already completed, which may include an original essay, a poem, a piece of art, a movie, or another creative work. Have a digital copy, file or photo ready to attach or include along with your activity sheet! It can't hurt.

For Parents

If there is anything you can do to support your student, manage the scholarship process. If your child doesn't have to work during school or take out more student loans, the benefits multiply. For instance, he or she may be able to maximize time off from school by participating in extension or internship opportunities that will enhance career opportunities upon graduation.

Use Worksheet 18: List of Real Scholarship Opportunities to keep track of scholarships for which you intend to apply and their deadlines. Select the most appropriate ones from both local offerings and Internet search results, such as from www.fastweb.com. Print and file submission requirements, if available, for easy reference.

You need to be a scholarship machine. This is a numbers game; however, don't sacrifice quality for quantity. Keep in mind that there are quite a few scholarships for which no one or nearly no one applies, which increases dramatically your odds of winning.

Point to Ponder

On the surface, it may appear easier to just sign for a few more student loans than to waste time applying for scholarships; however, it won't be too much fun to make those monthly student-loan payments for the next 10 years after you graduate. No one ever says, "I wish I would've taken out more loans."

Worksheet 18: List of Real Scholarship Opportunities

Scholarship Name	Official Website Address	Specific Requirements	Deadline

Loans and Work-Study Programs

The U.S. Department of Education manages the Direct Loan System, which transfers loan funds directly to colleges and universities for students' educational expenses. The Federal Perkins Loan Program is specifically designed to assist students with exceptional financial need through direct lending by colleges and universities. Detailed information about both federal loan programs is provided on the official website, www.studentaid.ed.gov.

> **Requirement**
>
> *Male* students must register with Selective Service at http://www.sss.gov to be eligible for federal and some state student loan and grant programs.

After completing your financial-aid paperwork, you will receive a Student Aid Report (SAR), which summarizes your data and calculates your Expected Family Contribution (EFC) based on your resources. This information is shared with designated schools that will create a customized financial-aid package for you. For instance, you will receive more financial-aid support to attend an expensive private college than you will to attend your own state's publicly funded university.

> **Point to Ponder**
>
> Don't feel pressured to memorize loan options and programs. When you receive an award letter from a college, you will have the opportunity to accept or reject specific loans and programs. Just remember that the lowest-interest loans are distributed to students who demonstrate the most financial need, which is calculated using personal financial and tax-return data, similar to Worksheet 16: Data Needed to Complete Net Price Calculator.

Federal Direct (Stafford) Subsidized loans are offered to undergraduate students who demonstrate financial need, usually represented by an adjusted gross income (AGI) of $100,000 or less on parents' tax returns. It is considered "subsidized" because the federal government pays interest while you are enrolled in school at least half-time and during the grace period, so your interest charges begin about six months after you graduate.

Federal Direct (Stafford) Unsubsidized loans are offered to both undergraduate and graduate students without the requirement to show financial need. You are responsible for paying or "accruing" interest charges while in school and during the grace period. This crucial difference between subsidized and unsubsidized loans is further explained at www.studentaid.ed.gov/types/loans/subsidized-and-unsubsidized.

Reminder

Colleges determine your total annual loan amount for both subsidized and unsubsidized loans. Repayment begins after a six-month grace period that begins after graduation or when your enrollment status is less than half-time. Monthly payments are calculated using total amount borrowed, interest rate, and repayment period of 10 years.

The Federal Perkins Loan Program provides funding to undergraduate, graduate, and professional students with demonstrated exceptional financial need through fixed-rate, low-interest loans. Not all colleges participate in this federal program, so check with Financial Aid Office staff. There is a set maximum loan program amount available annually to all students, so submit your FAFSA early to be considered for these limited funds. Check out www.studentaid.ed.gov/types/loans/perkins for current interest rates and eligibility requirements.

Federal (Parent) PLUS loans are available to parents of dependent students and graduate and professional students to pay for education expenses. There are eligibility requirements for applicants, which include a credit-history review. The maximum annual loan amount is calculated by subtracting financial aid received from the total cost of attendance. Loan terms include a fixed interest rate, higher than other federal loans, and additional fees. For the most up-to-date information on federal PLUS Loans, visit www.studentaid.ed.gov/types/loans/plus.

To accept a Federal PLUS loan, parents are required to complete the Direct Plus Loan Application and Master Promissory Note. The Education Department sends the loan money directly to the school to pay tuition, room and board, and other fees. If excess funds remain, they are released to the parent or student to pay for other student expenses.

Private loans are not funded by the federal government, but are made by a lender such as a bank or credit union. Private loans offer the least favorable terms, such as higher, variable interest rates and no deferment or grace period. They are often considered a last-resort option for financial aid. To learn more about the comparison of federal and private loans, visit www.studentaid.ed.gov/types/loans/federal-vs-private.

Federal work-study programs provide jobs to undergraduate and graduate students who demonstrate financial need. Positions, either on or off campus, pay at or above federal minimum wage directly to students who use the money to pay education expenses.

Hours assigned and money earned cannot be greater than the amount awarded for federal work-study (FWS) as listed on your financial-aid award letter. Financial-aid administrators are mindful of your class schedule and academic progress while enrolled in this program.

Point to Ponder

All federal loans and programs are optional. Upon receiving your financial-aid award letter, you will be able to accept or reject each loan and program type, item by item. By completing your financial-aid paperwork early, but only after January 1st, you maximize your opportunities—no commitments.

Free Application for Federal Student Aid (FAFSA)

To apply for federal financial aid, including government loans and grants, and scholarships, you must complete the Free Application for Federal Student Aid (FAFSA) at www.fafsa.ed.gov as soon as possible after January 1st. Forms are completed annually to apply for and receive financial aid for each year you are enrolled in school.

The U.S. Department of Education's website at http://studentaid.ed.gov/fafsa is the official guide for FAFSA instructions and support.

Point to Ponder

There are many websites offering advice and support related to financial aid. For instance, FinAid.org helps student and parents with financial-aid analysis by providing default and total debt statistics at www.finaid.org/loans.

Beware of websites that offer services-for-hire to assist you with the financial-aid process and applications. It is not necessary! There are great, free guides available to you and your parents at your guidance office and local library. Use your greatest resource by speaking with your guidance counselor about specific issues and concerns.

Request a PIN by selecting Apply Now on the official website at www.pin.ed.gov (notice the official .gov web address extension) during the fall of your senior year. You and your parents will each need a personal identification number (PIN) that acts as your digital signature when accessing and submitting FAFSA forms using the Internet.

FAFSA on the Web Worksheet and additional resources are provided by the Department of Education's website at www.studentaid.ed.gov/fafsa. Locate the link to the PDF version of the FAFSA on the Web Worksheet. Use this document to organize and compile the required information necessary to complete and submit your FAFSA on the Web, which includes recent tax returns, bank statements, investment records, and other personal and financial data.

Access the annual version of the FAFSA after January 1st at www.fafsa.ed.gov; follow the Start Here link.

Tip

The IRS Data Retrieval Tool is a new feature designed to assist FAFSA filers in viewing and securely transferring their recently filed tax-return data between systems.

Take time to look up federal school codes so you are ready to enter them on your FAFSA to indicate your decision to provide these schools with your results. The official FAFSA website at www.fafsa.ed.gov provides a search engine to look up federal school codes and other comparative statistics by state/location and school name.

The Student Aid Report (SAR) summarizes data entered on your FAFSA. You are offered the opportunity to reenter or correct information that will be shared with colleges as a means to calculate your individualized financial-aid package.

Tip

Expect to receive email from FederalStudentAidFAFSA@cpsemail.ed.gov related to your financial-aid application and SAR, as well as admissions office requests and online portal instructions from colleges. Check your Spam and Junk Mail folders frequently throughout this process, just in case.

Expected Family Contribution (EFC) is calculated by the Department of Education using information from the FAFSA. This amount used to calculate your eligibility for federal student financial aid appears as a separate item on your SAR.

FAFSA4caster is a free financial-aid calculator offered on the Department of Education's website at www.studentaid.ed.gov/fafsa/estimate. Follow a link to this tool, which estimates your eligibility for federal financial aid. However, do not rely on any estimates or expectations. Your financial-aid award letters, which you will receive in the spring, are the real thing.

CSS/Financial Aid PROFILE collects preliminary personal financial information about you and your family during the fall application process, after October 1st. This fee-based service provides a report that can be used by certain colleges to assist them in awarding school aid. Follow the link at https://profileonline.collegeboard.org/prf/index.jsp to view a listing of colleges that use CSS/PROFILE. However, the college's official website or admissions office staff are always the best source for the most accurate information and requirements.

Point to Ponder

Some colleges have a "need-blind" policy in which applying for financial aid does not impact admissions decisions. Other schools do not; they are considered "need-aware," and the ability to pay may be a factor in the decision. Don't forget to visit financial-aid webpages on each college's official website for more information about their policies, programs, and deadlines.

Reference Sheet F:
Financial-Aid Process Checklist

☐ Search for scholarship opportunities, both local and national.

☐ Complete CSS/PROFILE in the fall, only if required.

☐ Apply for scholarships.

☐ Visit and review each college's Financial Aid web pages.

☐ Speak with or email Financial Aid Office staff to discuss your options and special circumstances.

☐ Complete and submit FAFSA after January 1st.

☐ Search and apply for more scholarships.

☐ Review your Student Aid Report (SAR) to check for accuracy. Correct amounts if necessary.

☐ Receive financial-aid award letters from colleges.

☐ Analyze the elements of your financial-aid packages.

☐ Decide which financial-aid items(s) you want to accept.

☐ Accept an admissions offer and financial aid award by stated deadlines.

View the updated Student PROFILE Guide and begin the PROFILE requirement by accessing https://profileonline.collegeboard.org. You will be required to sign in with your CollegeBoard username and password, as noted on Worksheet 4: Login/Password Organizer.

Determine which schools require the PROFILE to be submitted by the application deadline—it should be listed in each school's application requirements. Do not send a PROFILE report to schools that don't ask for it! Please note that there are fees associated with processing and sending PROFILE results.

Cautionary Tale

We were shocked when we received the financial-aid award letter from our daughter's top-choice school. We didn't get nearly as much as we needed. I wrote a detailed letter to the financial-aid department head explaining the special circumstances of our situation, and guess what? They gave us more aid. We wound up paying less out-of-pocket for a private university than her friends who paid for state college.

—Ronnie B., freshman parent, anonymous university, New York

Pep Talk

It is important for you to own this process for many reasons. Firstly and most importantly, you are truly starting your life's journey by embracing adulthood with a vested interest in the plan as well as the outcome. There is nothing more demoralizing than when a student reports, "My parents did everything for me." On the surface, it may appear that parents are helpful and providing, but it may cause the student to become disconnected from the experience by not providing input into plan formation, application preparation, and decision-making processes.

When you manage the overall application process with assistance from your parents, it allows you to handle a situation that is similar to ones you'll experience while at college. Some students are stressed during the application process, which can be caused by fear of not meeting deadlines. When you take control of time management, create a plan, and feel confident about your abilities, your stress levels decrease. Often a lack of preparation causes stress. The application process allows you to showcase your skills and abilities while still under the supervision of your parents. Share the requirements and deadlines with your parents, so they can monitor and help out if needed.

For Parents

This is a great opportunity to observe your student's organizational abilities and time-management skills. When they are disorganized, students may not work effectively or efficiently because they are scattered, wasting energy to bring the pieces of the puzzle together in an orderly fashion. Parents, you can step in to create filing systems, binders, folders, and a dedicated work area. While in college, students will rely on organizational skills to manage academic assignments and financial records. These vital skills will also contribute to success into adulthood and their chosen career fields.

So, parents, during this crucial time in your student's life, it is important for you to establish a framework of success around this project. There are several opportunities where parents can be proactive, including proofreading applications, essays, and supplemental materials. Students often do not possess the critical eye needed to locate spelling and grammatical mistakes and the occasional typographical error.

Parent involvement is considered necessary when completing financial-aid forms and scholarship applications. Applying for financial aid using the FAFSA is straightforward but not easy, because you need to locate and report a ton of financial data. However, once you complete the FAFSA and CSS/PROFILE, if necessary, you will be better organized for next year. On the other hand, outside scholarship applications have individual requirements, with small print and varying deadlines. There are more than 50,000 scholarships offered to undergraduate students alone—so much money out there waiting, much of it unclaimed! Help your student claim all he or she can!

PART VI
Theirs and Yours

You have been making decisions throughout this process. You are confident: You've decided on a career path, you've decided which schools to apply to, you've completed financial-aid and scholarship applications. In life, you make and are affected by decisions every day. As we approach the end of the college selection process, your path will be affected by two decisions: theirs and yours.

You might be worried because your choice of colleges may be impacted by the admissions committees' decisions. Nurture a positive attitude; be hopeful that your expectations will be met. On the other hand, do not be fearful of the decisions you will soon make. You have worked very diligently to create a plan that is mindful of your interests, abilities, and academic achievements. You have considered your financial and familial obligations and limitations. Through effort, research, and observation, you will obtain the final bits of information necessary to allow you to easily determine which college to attend in the fall. Have faith in yourself and confidence in your abilities. Breathe.

Chapter 12
Their Decisions

After I submitted all my supplemental forms, I finally felt relieved. I'm so glad it's over and that I'll be getting my decisions soon instead of waiting until the spring. I think all my hard work definitely paid off, so now I can relax for the rest of the year.

—Ashley M., early action applicant

College admissions officers inform applicants of their decisions in several ways. Some send letters or packets to students using standard U.S. Postal Service mail, others use email notification, and still others use systems that allow students to log in through an online portal. No matter which way you get it, be prepared to receive a decision from most regular decision–deadline schools by early April.

- **Accepted.** Congratulations! They want you; they really want you. However, you should consider waiting until you receive decisions and financial-aid packages from all colleges before committing.

- **Waitlisted.** You didn't quite meet the requirements, but you aren't out of it yet. You were close, so they're going to let you know if they can squeeze you in once they learn which other applicants are accepting their offers. However, you must notify the admissions office that you are continuing on as a waitlist candidate.

> **Tip**
>
> Don't just sit back and wait for a "waitlisted" school. Move on with life by accepting admission at your next best college. That way if things don't work out, you are still set with a plan!

- **Deferred.** You're a borderline candidate, so Admissions is holding off on making a decision until they receive additional data either from you or from other applicants.

Point to Ponder

If you have been waitlisted or deferred from your top-choice school, it's time for action; don't sit back and pout. Get on the phone with your college admissions contact and express your interest explicitly! Ask a different teacher or professional to write a very specific and personalized letter to support your candidacy. Meet with your guidance counselor to develop a proactive plan that includes sending your quarterly and mid-year grades. Fight for your cause!

■ **Rejected.** Sorry, but you didn't meet the requirements set for the incoming freshman class. If rejection letters are starting to pile up, schedule an immediate appointment with your guidance counselor to adjust your plan.

Point to Ponder

You *should* expect to be rejected from one or two of the colleges on your list. This shows that you didn't underestimate your qualifications. You've tested the market and know where you stand.

Earning acceptances from two or more colleges is a wonderful feeling. You've made it! You're going to college! Now which one should you choose? They're all strong schools in one way or another; that's why you added each to your list.

You don't have to make a decision immediately, but you *do* need to gather more data to assist you in the process.

Campus Safety

Campus safety is an often-overlooked consideration during the college application and selection process. Previously it was a challenge to accurately assess the safety of a college campus. Even when visiting a campus with your parents, it's not easy to identify the "culture of safety." The Clery Center for Security on Campus, Inc. at www.securityoncampus.org, a nonprofit organization, pursued the rights of parents and students to be notified, and ultimately forewarned, of the types and prevalence of crimes occurring on and near campus.

To access the college-specific crime statistics, visit the Office of Postsecondary Education's Campus Safety and Security Data Analysis Cutting Tool website at http://ope.ed.gov/security. Follow the Get Data for One Institution/Campus link and search by the name of the college—keep it as simple as possible.

History

The Clery Center for Security on Campus was founded by a mother and father whose college-student daughter, Jeanne, was a victim of violent crime on campus. The investigation discovered a pattern of crimes committed on campus, of which both students and parents were unaware. Mr. and Mrs. Clery contended that students, including their daughter, would be better able to protect themselves and their property if they were aware of crimes committed on or near campus. Through their efforts, federal law now requires colleges participating in and receiving direct student aid to report accurate annual crime statistics and issue warnings to students and staff.

Before selecting the link to the college or campus, please note the total student enrollment at the school. This figure will be required to assess the culture of safety and student behavior at the college when we compare it to the number of crimes committed on or near campus.

Research answers to the following questions for each school you are considering. Locate and follow links to criminal offenses, hate crimes, arrests, disciplinary actions, and fire statistics categories.

- In each category, which are the most prevalent incidents on campus during the last three years?

- Consider what steps can you take to protect yourself and your property?

- Do you see an upward or downward trend in certain areas?

- Total disciplinary actions often reflect the college's culture towards student behavior. What do the statistics reveal about the school?

- Which reported categories and corresponding quantities concern you and your family?

- Comparing total incidents to the total enrollment, do you believe the campus has an overall culture of safety and security?

Blue Light Emergency Phone Systems are a network of telephone centers located across campus. Units are placed around buildings, walkways, and parking facilities and are easily identifiable by the blue light on the top of each one. These campus-wide phones are immediately and directly connected to university security or police via speaker phone. In case of an emergency or threat, a passerby can press the large button to alert and communicate with authorities; in response, university security personnel may be immediately dispatched to the scene. Print out or obtain a campus map to verify the locations of these emergency units.

College visits are important, since they play a role in the whole "fit" process. Some students will automatically know if they will fit in at the college as soon as they set foot on campus. The campus visit is also a good time to make your first impression and to interview for admissions. Interviews are great, since they give students the opportunity to express concerns with admissions about their application, etc. They also give the student (not the parent) time to ask questions about the college that they weren't able to find the answers to on their own.

—Emmanuel Cruz, Admissions Counselor, Hartwick College, New York

Note

The availability and quantity of Blue Light phones are often used to highlight the university's commitment to the safety of students and staff. However, there is no substitution for awareness and a personal commitment to ensuring your *own* safety.

Campus safety services are often provided and promoted to students and staff. Depending on the size of the campus, no-cost shuttle buses often follow the same circuitous route, stopping at academic buildings, student facilities, and residence halls. Most systems are restricted to students only, requiring riders to show university-issued identification. Check with the college's website for hours of operation and route.

In addition to shuttles, campus groups will often offer escorts to students who need or choose to walk across campus alone, especially at night. Students may need to call ahead to arrange for a buddy who will accompany them to their destination.

Good to Know

University of Florida's Student Nighttime Auxiliary Patrol (SNAP) provides nightly escorts anywhere on campus to persons on request. The service is staffed by students equipped and supervised by the university police department. A person requesting an escort may contact SNAP via telephone. The requester provides his or her first name and location of pickup and destination to the dispatcher, who determines the best method of meeting the requester's need. A walking or driving escort is dispatched to his or her location.[1] Similar services are available on most college campuses across the country. Check with the university's security or police department for details.

---

[1] www.universityparent.com/ufl/2009/04/06/university-of-florida-police-department.

College students soon become accustomed to traveling in groups, especially to evening activities such as socializing, studying at the library, or grabbing a bite to eat. There is a certain safety in numbers. Remember, if you decide to separate from the group, take advantage of the university's safety services. **Your personal safety is of the utmost importance to you, your family, and university staff.** It is the foundation for having a great college experience, excelling in your studies, and achieving your goals.

> *I chose my school because it has a city feel with a diverse lot of professors and students. The biggest factor was the fact that it is rated #18 as far as undergrad business schools go.*
>
> —**Mike H., Boston University, Massachusetts**

Retention and Graduation Rates

Retention rates report how many students return to study at a college after they complete freshman year. This speaks volumes about a college; if the retention rate is low, students are not committed to the education and experience on campus. A higher retention rate reflects the positive outcome of others, which should give you confidence about the on-campus environment as it relates to academics, social opportunities, and living arrangements.

You can view this powerful statistic on the NCES governmental website at http://nces.ed.gov/collegenavigator, where you can view the retention and graduation rate statistics by college.

Cautionary Tale

I wasn't a great student in high school. My average was in the high 70s, and my SAT scores were pretty low, but I played a varsity sport and was a good athlete. I didn't have the grades to go away to a state school, but I did get accepted to a small but expensive college out of state. I lasted one year there before transferring to community college back home. Even though the campus was beautiful, something wasn't right, and I didn't really like it there. Ms. Portnoy looked up the retention rate, and it was about 65 percent. If I had known, I definitely would've wondered why. I guess there were a lot of students who felt like I did.

—Anonymous community college student

Graduation rates report what percentage of students in a certain class year earn their degree within a specific time period—usually 150 percent of normal time for their program. Again, the NCES website provides very clear and easy-to-find statistics.

Most importantly, graduation rates show the culture of the school and students' attitudes toward academics. You can deduce whether students are merely starting off at a college and then choosing to transfer—or, worse yet, dropping out without finishing their studies. The higher the graduation rate, the more comfortable you should feel about investing your money and your efforts toward earning that degree.

Campus Visit

The campus visit is the most important piece of information in the college decision-making process. Some students and their families choose to visit colleges early, beginning junior year or before. Others travel during summer, especially between junior and senior year, for a family road trip to tour college campuses. To conserve time and financial resources, use weekends and school vacations during senior year to visit campuses, especially to schools where you have been accepted.

Junior Year

If you and your family have never had the opportunity to visit college campuses, any time is a great time to introduce yourself to various settings and characteristics, which include campus size, dorm-room choices, library and academic buildings, athletic facilities, and surrounding communities, which include urban, suburban, and rural settings. This early exposure to many campuses will build your background knowledge and familiarity of colleges in general. If you would like to recall the details of these trips for next year, take plenty of digital photos and notes of your opinions and impressions.

Summer

Again, any exposure to college campuses allows you to have a storehouse of data to compare potential choices. If the occasion arises, take advantage of all opportunities to visit campuses, including public and private institutions nearby and farther away.

Point to Ponder

The most important aspect of a college campus is the students. You must visit schools when classes are in session; this does not include the summer months, which unfortunately are usually the most convenient for family travel. You get a lot of information from current college students, including the clothes they wear, how they interact with each other, where they socialize, and so on. Another great indicator of student satisfaction is how they interact with a prospective student—you—when you tell them you are applying to their school. Interact—you will find that their excitement or apathy will tell you a lot.

The hardest transition of college is probably getting used to all the new and different people you meet and the new large lecture classes. I'm in a class of 115 in my History 200 class.

—Patrick F., SUNY Cortland, New York

Senior Year

Fall of senior year is hectic, between preparing for SATs and ACTs, completing applications and supplemental materials, and mastering required coursework. It may not be the best time to travel away from home, potentially missing valuable class time. Stay focused: It's time to take action and make mindful decisions about your future.

Spring of senior year is probably the most appropriate time to visit colleges, especially because your list is focused on schools where you have been accepted. Also, knowing you have already gotten in to these schools gives you a certain amount of confidence and a critical eye when looking at and comparing colleges.

> **Tip**
>
> Don't visit colleges too early on Saturday mornings. Most students are sleeping in, so you'll miss most of the action if you do. If you can manage it, schedule your visit on a day when students are attending classes, because you can get a real feel for what's happening on campus.

I am living in an all-freshman dorm and am lucky enough to have one of the biggest rooms. I live in a quad, which means that there are four of us in a room that is twice the size of everyone else's.

—Richie O., Siena College, New York

Additionally, by spring of your senior year, you'll have ample background knowledge and exposure with which to examine and critique your college choices. Knowing the final decision is only moments away, you really must use all of your senses and abilities to consider your options. And most importantly, you will have received your financial-aid awards, which puts a taste of reality into the final contenders.

> **Cautionary Tale**
>
> During the whole process, I planned to attend a pricey private university. It was in the final hour, when I really looked at how much money I would need to take out in student loans, that I changed my mind. How could I strap myself with more than $50,000 in student-loan debt, just for my bachelor's degree?
>
> —Anonymous commuter student

Worksheet 19:
College Visit Questionnaire

Use this worksheet to consider and record your observations for each college you visit. Make sure to take notes and photos, because after you visit a few schools, they will all blend together.

1. Where is the location of campus in relation to your home?

2. Is there access to mass transit/carpooling opportunities?

3. Is the campus setting urban, suburban, or rural?

4. What is the approximate size of the campus in area or acres?

5. What is the total student population—undergraduate and graduate?

6. Do you notice a feeling of community and interconnectedness on and around the campus?

7. Do you notice a feeling of belonging among the student body?

8. What is the quantity and comprehensiveness of libraries, books, and research facilities, including hours of operation?

9. What is the availability and quality of computer/technology equipment and facilities, including hours of operation?

10. What are the choices and quality (clean/spacious/updated) of dorm rooms and residence halls for freshmen? Upperclassmen?

11. What are the locations and options for dining halls, including food types and hours of operation?

12. Are there alternate dining facilities, using meal plans/points, surrounding campus?

13. Notice the prevalence of Blue Light Emergency Phones and campus police or security. Do you have accurate knowledge of campus safety and crime statistics?

14. Which campus security services are available, including shuttles and buddy/escort services?

15. Do you have knowledge of the surrounding community, town, or city, including safety concerns and local attractions?

16. Do you find the campus to be visually appealing with regard to layout and architecture?

17. What is the quality and availability of a fitness center, gym, athletic facilities, and a stadium?

18. Are professors accessible and approachable with posted office hours and locations?

19. What are the largest classes by number of students? Which classes are offered in this large, lecture hall format?

20. What is the process for course scheduling/registration each semester?

21. What is the quality and quantity of program-specific facilities, such as labs, studios, and theaters?

22. Which academic support services are offered to students?

23. Which health services/healthcare/emergency hotline/support services are offered to students?

24. Does it feel like home? Can you see yourself walking around campus? Living there?

For Parents

The college visit is a great time for you to be a participant and an observer, as both are required during the event. It's important for you to be a participant when your student needs to arrange travel and hotel plans, locate the admissions office, and sign up for the tour. There are also some very important parent-specific questions that need to be addressed regarding campus safety, financial aid, the surrounding community, and so on.

The college visit also offers a great opportunity to observe your student in this new environment, which may or may not be his or her new home in the near future. Ask yourself the following questions:

- Does your student actively engage and ask for directions and instructions when necessary?

- Does your student linger at the front or the back of the tour group?

- Does your student attach to you or buddy up with other prospective students?

- When unable to clearly hear a comment or question, does your student ask for it to be repeated?

- Does your student take notes or photos of campus?

- Does your student tell you not to ask any questions or embarrass him or her? If so, is he or she prepared to ask the necessary questions?

- Does your student arrive at campus with his or her own plan or agenda of buildings, facilities, and areas to explore?

- When the guided tour is over, does your student want to explore with you or on his or her own?

- Will your student ask current students questions about the college or campus?

- Would your student like to sit in on a college class or speak with a professor?

- How comfortable does your student look walking around campus? Is he or she actively engaged? Making eye contact? Smiling and excited?

Only you know your child, and only you can gauge how your child will adapt to life as a college student. There is no formula or calculation to predict your student's adjustment and satisfaction. It is an eye-opening experience to really see your child interact as a quasi-adult while still under your watchful eye and guidance.

For Parents

Chapter 13
Your Decision

Overall, college has been pretty good thus far, and I am certainly having a good time.

—Joe S., Penn State University, Pennsylvania

By early spring you will be ready to make your final decision, if you haven't done so already. There are scenarios where this opportunity will come both easier and earlier for some, including early-decision applicants, recruited athletes, students who are heart-set on a school, and those not totally reliant on financial-aid awards.

Many students are undecided about their college pick; they love two or three schools equally. Unfortunately, there is no formula for choosing the perfect college, but there are many colleges that will ultimately offer you a great experience, lifelong friends, and an education and preparation for an awesome career.

To make a well-informed decision, you need a few key pieces of information, including your acceptance letters, financial-aid award letters, notes and reflections on college visits, and personal input from you and your family.

To a certain extent, don't stress over it too much. You now have a choice to make— the first of many decisions that will direct the course of your life. And that is what it's all about—directing. In the future, there will always be another opportunity to adjust, change direction, or backtrack at the next crossroads. Be confident in yourself, your abilities, and the many great opportunities you will have.

To be honest, many students must make this decision based solely on the amount of financial aid offered. When judging the quality of financial-aid packages, don't forget to really focus on the scholarships and grants offered—they are considered gift aid and do not need to be repaid.

Finances can be a very big consideration in your final decision, but don't be swayed or forced to accept something just because it's cheaper or free. Be mindful of the decisions you make. Consider each factor, and if your financial position weighs heavily, then go for it!

Point to Ponder

If life circumstances are affecting you and/or your family, including financial, health, and/or personal issues, be smart. Stay local and cheap if that's what the current conditions require. There will be an opportunity or crossroads during the next two years where you will have the option to transfer and attend the college of your dreams, if you still desire.

Financial-Aid Award Letters

The federal government uses data submitted on your FAFSA to calculate your Expected Family Contribution (EFC). After applying their formula, they issue a Student Aid Report (SAR), which is sent to you and each school listed on your FAFSA.

Tip

Review all data carefully on your SAR. If there are any errors or omissions, log in to correct it immediately. Incorrect information will have a direct effect on your financial-aid programs and amounts.

Upon receipt, each college uses data reported on your SAR to develop a customized financial-aid package. The letter, which can be sent to you via mail or online portal, details elements that make up the total aid offered to you.

Your challenge is to decipher each award letter to determine the amount of gift aid (scholarships and grants) compared to money that needs to be repaid (government and private loans) plus your family's expected contribution. The information is there for you, but each school formats its letters and labels the amounts differently.

Use Worksheet 20: Financial-Aid Award Comparison to identify components of your financial-aid package as listed on your financial-aid award letter. Do not include outside scholarships from private companies, civic organizations, or foundations because most often you can use these at whichever college you attend.

Caution

Be aware of "front-loading" on your initial financial-aid award letters. This practice allows admission staff to entice you to enroll at their college with the lure of a large package, but with no guarantee that the financial-aid gift money will reoccur for sophomore, junior or senior years.

Worksheet 20:
Financial-Aid Award Comparison

College Name: **Award Letter Date:**

	Annual Amount Offered	Accept	Decline
Total Cost of Attendance (Use your Personalized TCOA as calculated on Worksheet 15)	$		
Federal Grants			
Additional Grants			
Scholarships			
Scholarships			
Awards			
Awards			
Add Total Gift Money:	= $		
Federal Work Study			
Federal Direct Subsidized Loans (Perkins/Stafford)			
Federal Direct Unsubsidized Loans (Stafford)			
Private Loans			
Federal PLUS Loans			
Add Total Loans Accepted:	= $		
Anticipated Annual Family Contribution (amount agreed to by your parents, not the SAR) includes student and educational savings monies	$		
Add Total Resources Expected (in bold):	= $		
Unaccounted Difference (TCOA – Total Resources Expected)	= $		

The unaccounted difference represents the amount of funds needed to fully cover the total cost of attendance (TCOA). Sources may include additional or increased loan amounts, outside scholarships, and higher family contributions.

Helpful websites for analyzing and decoding financial-aid award letters provide insight and exposure to the different layouts and terms used. Financial Aid Letter.com presents samples from a variety of colleges at www.financialaidletter.com. The site includes a tool that highlights "free" money, or gift aid, offered from each school.

> **Tip**
>
> Keep an eye out for the Federal Financial Aid Shopping Sheet. View a sample at www.collegecost.ed.gov/shopping_sheet.pdf. The aim is to standardize financial-award letters for all colleges. According to the White House, the Shopping Sheet is the culmination of a joint effort between the Consumer Financial Protection Bureau and the Department of Education to provide individuals with critical information about their financial decision to attend college in a clear, concise, and standardized format that facilitates easy comparisons across institutions. This is an individualized standard financial-aid award letter that will help students and families understand the costs of college before making the final decision on where to enroll.[1]

FinAid: The SmartStudent Guide to Financial Aid offers basic and advanced web-based Award Letter Comparison calculators at www.finaid.org/calculators/awardletter.phtml to assist in your analysis of up to three college's offers. The U.S. Government's Consumer Financial Protection Bureau's new tool at www.consumerfinance.gov/payingforcollege/ allows you to perform an apples-to-apples comparison of award letters. They also offer additional support and information for students at www.consumerfinance.gov/students/.

> **Caution**
>
> As you take advantage of scholarship awards from outside the college or government, you are required to inform the financial-aid office of your receipts. There are laws that dictate the effects of these monies on your overall financial-aid package. Be sure to check with the financial-aid office at each college to determine their outside scholarship policy. However, this should *never* discourage your efforts to get as much scholarship money as possible.

Second reminder: To be eligible for financial aid each year, you and your family must file the FAFSA annually as soon as possible after January 1st. You will then receive an award letter detailing your aid package for the following school year.

---

[1] www.whitehouse.gov/blog/2012/07/24/new-shopping-sheet-will-make-it-easier-students-know-they-owe.

Caution

You can lose financial-aid funding, especially grants and scholarships. Some are dependent on you earning a minimum GPA, so if your grades drop, you jeopardize your financial resources.

If you and your family's financial situation, as reported on the FAFSA and SAR, change dramatically, your Expected Family Contribution and aid package will change accordingly.

Athletes must also realize that sports scholarships are not guaranteed; they are performance-based or "pay-to-play." If you are injured, are unable to play, or choose not to play, you may lose your funding.

Be aware that some grants and scholarships are awarded on a one-time basis only. It is crucial for you to know which aid repeats or renews annually. Ask specific questions!

In our ever-changing world, it is important for you to have a realistic awareness of your situation if you were to lose access to financial aid for whatever reason. Would you take out more loans, if available? Or transfer to a cheaper school? Or finish your degree as a commuter student while living at home?

Rank Them

Use Worksheet 21: Rank Them: Pro or Con to compare two colleges you "got into" and are seriously considering. You may need additional copies of this worksheet to compare and rank three or more schools by comparing two and then moving the winner on to compete against others, like a playoff.

> *I chose my college based on the fact that I didn't get into my first choice and all of the other schools I had been accepted to were extremely expensive, even with financial aid and scholarships.*
>
> **—Chelsea R., CUNY Manhattan Community College, New York City**

Some students are comfortable relying on their gut reaction. Many report that they knew which campus to choose after spending 15 minutes on campus. It was something about the vibe and the people. The worksheet is recommended either way; it can always support what you know in your heart.

Worksheet 21:
Rank Them: Pro or Con

Method 1: Write the term "Pro" or "Con" in each of the columns to describe how you rate features/opportunities at each school. Use "Pro" if the school presents a positive outlook and "Con" for a negative or poor one. If an item is of particular importance to you and your family, circle your answer.

Method 2: Write either "Yes" or "No" for each criterion, depending on which school presents the best option. You can substitute "High" or "Low" or even "Good" or "Bad," as long as one school has the clear advantage. Again, if an item is of particular importance to you and your family, circle your answer.

Add your own personal or program-specific criteria in the blanks.

When finished, your preferences will become more apparent.

Name of school		
Reputation/prestige/selectiveness level		
Academic opportunities, including availability of majors and support services		
On-campus housing options		
Campus setting and surrounding community		
Distance from home		
Estimated total cost of attendance		
Scholarship and grants *offered*		
Student loans and work-study *required*		
Athletic opportunities		
College-visit feedback		
Parental feedback		

Final Date of Decision: Universal May 1st Deadline

Before you make your final decision, calculate your expected monthly loan payments. It is an eye-opening experience. Remember, it's really easy to sign a loan document or promissory note and worry later about paying. In reality, later arrives really quickly—usually just about the same time you want to buy a new car, rent an apartment, or take a vacation.

You can use a standard auto-loan calculator or FinAid: The SmartStudent Guide to Financial Aid's loan calculator at www.finaid.org/calculators/loanpayments.phtml. Calculate the estimated monthly loan payment for each type of loan as interest rates vary, using the standard term loan of 10 years for all loan types.

Be mindful of financial-aid acceptance deadlines. Stay in contact with financial-aid office staff for assistance and clarification of terms and programs.

By May 1st, National Enrollment Confirmation Day, you are required to send a deposit to one college, declaring your intention to attend. Waitlisted students may have the opportunity to send an additional deposit once notified of their acceptance, but they are required to immediately inform the other school and may forfeit that initial deposit.

Use Worksheet 22: Estimated Total Loans and Monthly Payments to calculate your total student loans and resulting monthly payments. You can also estimate similar totals for loans taken out by your parents.

> **Note**
>
> Most loans require a $50 minimum monthly payment regardless of the loan balance.

> **Caution**
>
> It is unwise to let your total student loan debt be greater than the starting salary of your intended career. For example, the national average starting salary for an elementary school teacher is $31,000 per year. How do the financial commitments of your college choices compare to this benchmark?

Remember that this is only an estimate; actual amounts will vary. Here are a few reasons why: First, it may take you longer than four years to graduate. Second, you may need to take out more money in loans during later years due to increases in tuition. Finally, unsubsidized and private loans accrue (charge) interest while you are in school, even though you (or your parents) may or may not choose to make payments during that time.

Worksheet 22: Estimated Total Loans and Monthly Payments

Loan Type For You:	Annual Amount	Multiplied By	Total Amount	Estimated Monthly Payment (as determined by loan calculator results)
Federal Stafford Direct Loans (use actual or 6.8% interest rate)		× 4* years		
Federal Perkins Direct Loans (use actual 5% interest rate)		× 4 years		
Unsubsidized Stafford Loans (use actual 6.8% interest rate)		× 4 years		
Private Loans (use actual rate as stated on loan document)		× 4 years		
Other		× 4 years		
Total Estimated Student Loans			**$**	
Loan Type For Your Parents:				
PLUS Direct Loans (use actual or 7.9% interest rate)		× 4 years		
Other		× 4 years		
Total Estimated Parent Loans			**$**	

* You can adjust the number of years or total loan amounts according to your specific program or degree requirements.

Most students remit the required documents and deposit before May 1st. This may be an advantage when requesting on-campus housing, because the office of residential life assigns dorms and rooms based on the date of receipt of the housing deposit.

Because many regular-deadline schools do not release admissions decisions until April, some students don't have the opportunity to decide much earlier, but that's fine because all applicants are in the same situation.

I was torn between my top two schools, so I made my decision based on the best financial-aid package offered. I sent in my deposit and enrollment forms by the May 1st deadline and got a call from the other school a few days later. They knew I was really interested in their school and offered to increase their financial aid to me. It put me in an awkward position, but I changed my mind. Now I am really happy with my final, final decision.

—Jessica H., Marist College, New York

Take advantage during the weeks prior to the May 1st universal deadline to contact the financial-aid officers and admissions staff to ask them to identify any additional financial-aid opportunities available to you.

Don't forget that the admissions staff has worked very hard all year to offer admission to the very best candidates, including you! You are now in a position of power, ready to spend tuition dollars at the college of your choice. Don't forget that!

Once you're committed, it is highly recommended and greatly appreciated for you to inform the other colleges that you will not be attending their esteemed university. Your decision may open the door for a few waitlisted students to take those spots that you no longer need or want.

Congratulations on a job well done!

Throughout my senior year, everybody would always give their advice on which school I should go to for which specific reasons. It is important for seniors to remember that this is their decision and that they should try not to take unsolicited advice. You can listen to what people have to say and take it into consideration, but with a grain of salt. Everyone is going to have a different college experience, so do not make a decision just because someone said to. Not only will parents be advising you, but friends, family members, and even faculty will be eager to help and be involved in this important time of your life. And you should be thankful that so many people want to see you succeed in life, but you need to make sure the decision you make is the best one for you. You want to choose the college that is best for you and because you want to go there.

—Courtney F., Hofstra University, New York

PART VII
Success on Campus

There are so many wonderful and exciting opportunities for you to experience over the next few years. Independent living, social events and parties, trips and new life-long friends are the hallmark of college. Final exams, midterms and research papers, all-nighter studying sessions, GPA calculations, money management and maintaining personal relationships are the anticipated stressors.

No one can really prepare you for what you will endure during these years, but there are some topics that can be previewed. The following chapters will expose you to some of the opportunities, responsibilities and hazards that you and your college friends may encounter. Keep the lessons and words of wisdom shared by others in mind as you go.

Chapter 14
Topics to Anticipate

The most important thing to me was finding a roommate, rather than letting the school assign me one. Once you start making your final decision, start looking people up on Facebook. Most of the schools have a page (usually made by an incoming freshman), and it is an easy way to find people who you think you may have a lot in common with. Although you may feel uncomfortable, everybody else is in the very same position that you are in.

—**Richie O., Siena College, New York**

What an exciting time! The pressures of planning and decision-making are behind you, and now it's excitement all the way. Get yourself a great college T-shirt or sweatshirt and wear it with pride. Finish your senior year with consistent grades and a positive attitude, and the school year and summer will fly by. Enjoy!

Orientation

College orientation is a comprehensive program designed to welcome students and their families to school. It is a high-energy, activity-packed experience that introduces you to fellow students, available services, and campus facilities and features.

Each college structures its orientation program differently. Some schools invite incoming freshmen—that's you—to spend a night or two or a week at campus during June, July, or early August. Other schools schedule their orientation programs immediately prior to the start of classes. Either way, it will be jam-packed with events, activities, and possibly off-campus adventures.

Most often during summer orientation programs, you're expected to stay in a dorm with other students. Even if you're considered a "commuter" student who lives at home, most colleges prefer you to stay on campus to experience orientation and get a feel for campus.

Orientation events and dates of availability are scheduled on first-come, first-served registration. Read terms and restrictions carefully, as some colleges charge a fee for the event.

Your orientation team's goal is for you to connect with students, staff, and college community. Admissions staff and college administrators are aware that freshman-retention rate is an important factor that affects their reputation. Accordingly, a considerable amount of time and energy is invested in creating phenomenal programs to establish confidence and trust for both students and their parents.

Possible orientation topics and responsibilities, scheduled for students and parents together and separately, may include:

- Opening remarks/welcome reception
- Campus tours
- ID photo/card
- Health and wellness
- Alcohol and drug awareness/prevention
- Residence halls and advisors
- Placement tests
- Advisement and course registration
- Meals, barbecues, and dances
- Games and contests
- Fire and campus safety
- Movies and concerts
- Commuter students
- Campus academic and health services

Be prepared to participate in fun activities and icebreakers. Be open to new friends and experiences. Leave your "too cool for school" and negative attitudes at home. Don't be a wallflower; break out of your shell! If the unknown is driving you crazy, search for "orientation schedule" on your school's official website to get a sneak preview.

Remember, everyone is in the same boat as you. No one has done this before. It makes sense for you to be nervous, but just change the name to "excitement" and have fun with it!

Point to Ponder

Many colleges offer adventure-style and community-service outings as part of an additional, "optional" orientation experience. These expeditions, based on team-strengthening skills, are meant to build student bonds/friendships to support the transition to college.

The dorms here are beautiful! A lot of my friends live in suites and have their own bathrooms. I live in a traditional double room. I share a bathroom with 15 girls, and we have 5 bathroom stalls, 8 sinks, and 4 showers. I have never had to wait for a shower or anything like that, which is really nice. (I hate having to wear flip-flops in the shower, though!) Our bathrooms are cleaned once every day except on Saturday and Sunday.

—Carli C., Quinnipiac University, Connecticut

College placement tests, often scheduled during orientation week, are given to incoming freshmen to identify potential areas of weakness in academic subjects. Results are then shared with your academic advisor, who guides you in creating your first semester's course schedule.

Caution

You will not be able to register for classes until you take the placement tests. And the earlier you take these tests, the more flexibility and opportunities may be available when selecting time slots, days, and even professors.

It is crucial for you to know when and where these placement tests are given, as you need to *prepare* for them. You need to review math formulas, grammar rules, and comprehensive reading skills. Don't blow this off! If you don't score well, you may have to take remedial or review courses in college.

Tip

Some students are exempt from taking placement tests based on high scores in math, critical reading, and writing sections of the SAT and ACT. Search for "placement tests" on your college's official website or contact the admissions office for details.

Many schools use College Board's ACCUPLACER computerized testing program as their method of assessment. You can find descriptions of exams and testing environment at www.collegeboard.com/student/testing/accuplacer. College Board also offers a test-prep app, sample questions, and tips for students. Additional test prep resources are available at www.testprepreview.com/accuplacer_practice.htm, as well as on many other websites. For the most specific and accurate information, search "placement tests" on your college's official website or speak with an admissions staff member. Great news: You can take advantage of the newly released official ACCUPLACER iTunes Study App, too!

Developmental courses are non-credit, mandatory courses that help students improve skills and achieve mastery. Be prepared to take at least two math courses in college, no matter which major you choose. Keep in mind that calculus is considered college-level math. If your high school math skills aren't up to par or you haven't taken pre-calculus, you may be required to take remedial math. The same goes for your writing and reading skills at the college level, so take it seriously.

Cautionary Tale

I bombed my math placement test. I was freaked out by being away from home and not knowing anybody. I was overwhelmed, and it was really hot. When I got my results, I couldn't believe it: remedial math. Throughout the course, I got straight As on every exam. Obviously I didn't need the extra help, but I still had to take the class.

—Darrin P., University of Delaware Alumnus

If you're mandated to take one, two, or even three remedial classes, it can affect your expected date of graduation. These remedial classes cost as much as regular college courses, but you don't earn credits for taking them. You may think this is unfair, but past experience shows that when skills are weak, the likelihood increases for students to fail. So instead of students struggling, and failing, college administrators prefer to be proactive about improving academic skills and abilities.

Meeting with your advisor or an admissions counselor is the next step in making your first-semester class schedule. There are several introductory classes that freshmen are required to take, which may include freshman composition (writing) and literature, as well as a math course. Most other course offerings are based on specific guidelines or degree requirements related to your intended major or general program of study. Make sure to bring a list of all Advanced Placement, IB, and college-credit bearing coursework that you have successfully completed to this appointment.

Tip

Take advantage of different class times to create a schedule mindful of your daily routines and preferences. Schedule early-morning classes if you plan to work or play a team sport, or select afternoon classes if you do better when well rested.

It's a little early in your college experience to choose classes based on the reputations of professors. Through conversations with classmates and helpful websites, such as Rate My Professors at www.ratemyprofessors.com, in the future you can incorporate other factors into your scheduling preferences.

Requirement

Be sure to have proper documentation signed by your physician as proof of immunization. State law requires colleges to have this on file before allowing you to register for classes.

Time Management

Most students understand the concept of time management and scheduling, in theory. You need to budget or allocate time to fulfill responsibilities, and if you do that well, you will have plenty of time for fun and entertainment.

In high school, most time-management requirements are limited to the present day or week. Students are reminded of their responsibilities often and usually complete and meet them prior to deadlines.

For example, high school teachers conduct review sessions to prepare students for tests and you may even *choose* to study by reviewing class-notes and assignments. The teacher likely reminds students all week about the scheduled exam, even writing a note on the board for all to see. In college, things are a bit more complex. You are expected to self-manage and be more independent, so there is a need for greater structure and awareness of events and timelines to prepare for exams and deadlines further in the future.

On the first day of class, your college professors will distribute a *syllabus* for each course that states the objective, required texts, grading criteria, and required assignments, which include projects, exams, and papers. A syllabus can be very detailed, including the exact dates of chapters covered, exams and due dates for papers and projects. Once the syllabus has been distributed, professors have given fair and written notice of the requirements, so no additional reminders are necessary or offered.

Cautionary Tale

When I walked into the classroom, I noticed everyone handing in a paper. I asked the girl next to me, "What's going on?" She told me that today was the due date of the research paper…according to "the syllabus." After class, I told the professor that I forgot my paper. He told me to go to the registrar's office to drop the class because I would never be able to get a passing grade with a ZERO on this assignment.

—Tricia M., Hofstra University alumna, New York

Additionally, there are fewer exams in college courses. Professors don't give a chapter test after each topic, but rather a unit exam on three or four chapters at once. It's nearly impossible to review all of the required notes and assignments only the night before the exam. In college, you will begin preparing and studying two, three, and sometimes four days before an exam, depending on the content and quantity of material covered.

To be properly prepared for all assignments in five or six different courses for the three- to four-month span of a semester, you must know what is required over the next month. Some students choose to organize this information electronically, while others stick with pens and paper planners. Each method is effective and efficient; what matters most is that you update your time-management tool and refer to it frequently.

Since, the syllabus is your professor's handbook for class, once you get it, you must identify and record each assignment's name and due date on your calendar. This way, you can determine time-management needs and requirements over the long term. In addition, you can see which are the busiest weeks, identify conflicts, and troubleshoot early on.

If you choose to use a planner or calendar as your time-management tool, make sure to bring it to class every day. That way, if there is a change or addition, you can update it immediately.

 Your planner or calendar must have a monthly view, not just daily or weekly. This gives you better perspective for long-term planning and oversight, which are needed in college.

Electronic or digital calendars are a great way to combine technology and time management. Students are totally attached to their cell phones, which is great for emergency purposes and keeping in close contact with friends and family. And now the Calendar function creates another really practical purpose for these smartphones.

For example, the Internet-based Calendar tool at www.google.com allows you to create an account using your current email address or Gmail log-in, if you have one. You can add events to the calendar, including birthdays and holidays, appointments, exams, work hours, project and paper due dates, and so on, which can even be color-coded by type or category.

To add a new event, double-click the date. A dialog box will open that asks for details, including event name, time, duration, location, color-code, and so on with an option to have it repeat annually, weekly, and so on.

After you save the event, it will appear on your calendar, which is available to you on any Internet-connected device, including laptops, smartphones, and tablet computers. Print the calendar as many times as you want, either by day, week, or month, to post and share it as needed.

> **Tip**
>
> As you add more events to your calendar, it will reflect a realistic picture of your time-management responsibilities. Use it to schedule your classes, work hours, fitness activities, and most importantly, study time. Set aside segments of time prior to exams, large projects, and finals.

Senior year is really not a time to stop doing work once you have been accepted to colleges. I slacked off a little bit during the fourth quarter (as everyone does), and I wish that I would have kept up with all of the readings my teachers assigned me (mostly English!). If there is one class that is going to help you excel in college, it is English by far; so if you want to slack off, then just keep working hard in your English class.

—Carli C., Quinnipiac University, Connecticut

Link the calendar to your smartphone so that everywhere you take your phone, you have your calendar. If you need, you can always refer to your schedule or even add to or change an event. Linking the two allows the phone and calendar to always be in sync!

Also, you can edit settings to receive text or email event reminders and a daily agenda each day. Be aware: Standard text-messaging rates may apply.

> **Caution**
>
> You can have all the time-management tools, calendars, Post-its, reminders, alarms, and so on, but if you don't respect them, you will find yourself in stressful situations, missing deadlines, unprepared, pulling all-nighters, and just not going to class.
>
> If this happens and your grades plummet, college administrators may put you on some type of academic probation or restriction. This is serious. The next step could possibly be expulsion, when they tell you not to return to school. Remember, colleges want students and graduates who excel, because it reflects well on their reputation, thereby improving enrollment numbers and raising admission criteria and standards.

Make sure you are organized even before classes begin, you know your requirements, and you allow yourself the time and opportunity to submit your best work!

Reference Sheet G lists instructions that will help you set up and use Google calendar. If you prefer another provider, expect similar features and steps.

Reference Sheet G:
Google Calendar Setup and Use

Create a Google Account Using Your Real Email Address or Use Your Gmail Account

1. Use your web browser and navigate to www.google.com.
2. Follow the link to Sign In (in the top-right corner).
3. Sign in with your existing Gmail or Google account, or
   a. Follow the link to Create an Account Now (in the bottom-right corner).
   b. Complete the required information—use your "real" primary email account.
   c. Follow the link to I Accept. Create My Account.
   d. Select Add This Webpage to the Home Page Tabs, if necessary.

View Google Calendar

1. Select More (on the menu bar) at Google.com.
2. Select Calendar.
3. Use the links to change the calendar view to Day, Week, Month, 4-Days, or Agenda.
4. Using the More drop-down menu, select Print, if desired.

Add Events to Google Calendar

1. Double-click on any date to open Add Event.
2. Add additional event features and settings:
   ▪ Untitled Event: To name your event.
   ▪ Dates: For events longer than one day.
   ▪ All Day (check box): When deselected, the time-frame option appears.
   ▪ Repeat (check box): When selected, options appear.
   ▪ Event Color (check box): Used to categorize or highlight events.
   ▪ Reminders: For notification settings.
   ▪ Add Guests: To send email invitations to others.

3. Click Save.

Customize Google Calendar Settings and Features

1. Click the Settings drop-down menu and select Settings.
2. On Calendar Setting page, select the General Settings link.
3. Update Personal Preference settings. You can personalize:
   - Default View
   - Weather
   - Time
   - Location/Zip Code
   - And so on
4. Click Save.

Mobile Setup for SMS Reminders

1. On Calendar Settings page, click the Mobile Setup link.
2. Enter the required information.
3. Receive text message updates/reminders on your cell phone. Standard rates apply.
4. Process the verification code.
5. Click Save.

Professors don't care about you unless you show an effort to care about their classes and work. Make sure they know your name. Attendance in most classes is a joke, but it can come back to bite you at the end of the semester if you don't go, so go to class. As long as you're there and the teacher knows that, you will get the better end of the stick.

—Andrew H., Towson University, Maryland

Roommates and Living Arrangements

For anyone who plans to live on campus, the idea of sharing a dorm room is scary. No matter whether it's a stranger or a friend, many students have never had to share a room or live in such close quarters with limited privacy.

Some freshmen decide to live with people they know from home, while others choose to find someone at orientation, and others let the university match them with appropriate roommates. None of these methods is a guarantee for blissful happiness, but they are all opportunities for personal growth.

The university-housing office attempts to identify compatible roommates based on the evaluation of your *Freshman Roommate Questionnaire*. Topics include sleeping routines, housekeeping style, musical tastes, study habits and preferences, extracurricular interests, attitudes toward diversity, and special circumstances and requests. A new high-tech tool used to identify a compatible roomie is a software or web-based matching assessment, such as WebRoomz, which uses more elaborate categories and questions.

Many students use Facebook and other websites to network with other incoming freshmen, especially those who are looking for roommates. Search for the official group "*College Name* Class of 20*XX*," where the year represents your expected college graduation date. The official site should be a closed group where administrators who work for the college approve each member, so you're assured of who you are talking to.

Introduce yourself, find others who will be at the same orientation session, and go from there. Always be aware of "stranger danger," but remember that at college you're going to meet many strangers who will become great friends.

Over the summer, you should contact your roommate(s) to figure out which items you intend to bring for your dorm room. Do you plan to color-coordinate bedding? Who will bring the TV? Do you need two printers? Who will rent the micro-fridge? Do you have a small rug for the floor?

On Move-In Day, if you arrive first, be mindful of creating a fair and friendly environment from the beginning. Don't take the best bed, location, and desk just because you got there first. If your roommate does that to you, set things straight immediately, because many horrible-roommate stories are just an accumulation of annoyances and small grievances. You're an adult; speak up for yourself. Don't take advantage, but don't be a sucker, either.

You and your roommate are a powerful team. You both, along with students from your hall, are a support system during the first weeks of school. As a group, you'll walk to the dining hall together, eat at the same table, and venture out to explore campus.

My roommate and I got off to a slow start because he went home every weekend to visit his girlfriend. But by the end of freshman year, we were close. We ended up living together all four years and are still great friends today.

—Darrin P., University of Delaware Alumnus

As the weeks go by, you will fine-tune your friendships as you meet students from other dorms, events, and your classes. While living together, it's important for you and your roommate to be on good terms, and this starts the moment you move in, if not sooner.

If things are going steadily downhill between you and your roommate(s), speak with your residence advisor (RA) to keep him or her updated on the issues. There are many programs and levels of assistance available to help you both create a more comfortable environment.

Caution

There are many rules and regulations that you must adhere to when living in a residence hall. Familiarize yourself with your school's policy, especially regarding prohibited items and causes for disciplinary actions.

By spring, you will have enough experience to decide with whom and where you want to live for your sophomore year, be it an on-campus dorm, an off-campus apartment, or a fraternity or sorority.

What to Bring to College

Getting ready to live on campus requires a lot of thought and preparation. You can look at it as if you are packing for a long vacation away from home—part camping trip and part hotel stay.

You should pack articles of clothing, including your favorite T-shirts, jeans, skirts, pants, and sweaters; shoes, boots, flip-flops, and sneakers; rain jackets, sweatshirts, coats, hats, and gloves; and workout clothes and a bathing suit.

Closet and storage space in a dorm room is limited, to say the least. If you go to a school where the climate is consistent, you're lucky that you don't have to worry about clothing for all four seasons. But if you don't, hopefully you can travel home once or twice during the semester to bring home certain items, swapping them out for the next season's necessities.

Bring necessary personal-hygiene supplies and accessories, including shampoo and conditioner, deodorant, hairdryer/appliances, makeup, contact lens supplies, shaving cream and razors, aspirin, cold and allergy medicine, and so on. A bathrobe and flip-flops or shower shoes allow you to walk to and from the bathroom/shower with modesty and cleanliness. Be prepared: This is not your house. There are a ton of people walking around the halls, in and out of rooms all the time, and your mom is not cleaning the facilities for you.

Have fun purchasing items to outfit and decorate your dorm room. You need extra shelving and storage, such as decorative milk crates or plastic cabinets with drawers. Caddies for toiletries and school supplies allow for easy transport and organization of your possessions.

Decorative wall hangings and a 4×6 area rug make your room a comfortable and personalized space. Expect the walls to be cinderblock or cement, so bring a variety of adhesive strips, such as Command products at www.command.com.

Tip Remember, most of these items should be considered throwaways, so don't spend a fortune, even though I still have my fluorescent-green milk crates from the early 1990s.

Most campuses provide rental microwaves and/or refrigerators approved for use in dorm rooms. It's great to store drinks and snacks, fresh fruit, and easy-to-prepare meals and leftovers. You may choose to grab a yogurt before going to your first class of the day and eat a leisurely breakfast afterwards. Your meal plan covers most of the meals you eat, but you still need drinks and snacks conveniently stored in your room. Remember to coordinate with your roommate to determine who will arrange for the rental.

Most parents don't purchase extra-long twin mattresses for their children, but most colleges do. This specialty size is narrower and longer than a traditional twin mattress, so you may need to purchase new bedding. Check with the residence-life office to verify your mattress size.

Most stores that sell bedding have a variety of styles in extra-long twin, so read labels carefully. Another interesting fact about college mattresses is that they are usually encased in a plastic covering, which protects them from contamination and spills, lucky for you. Think about buying a mattress pad or foam egg-crate to make it more comfy.

Along with bedding, you will need towels and washcloths, laundry detergent and baskets, and basic cleaning supplies. A small assortment of plates, bowls, cups, silverware, and mugs will allow you to dine in comfort when eating in your room.

Note Don't pack your belongings and clothes in suitcases. Large bags—even garbage or contractor bags—are perfect because there's no place to store luggage after you unpack. Also, those empty bags will be useful down the road when you need to clean up or even move out.

> **Tip**
>
> In college, you will do your own laundry once a week at most. Be prepared by having many pairs of socks and underwear as well as plenty of towels to get you through to your next "laundry day." Also, don't leave your favorite sweatshirts unattended in the dryer because sometimes they aren't there when you come back to get your clothes.

In addition to having a microwave/fridge in your dorm room, most residence halls are equipped with a common kitchen area, which may include a full-sized sink, oven, stove, and refrigerator—some even come with pots and pans. However, don't leave anything too valuable in this area, which is prone to "unauthorized sharing."

When you arrive on campus, ready to move in, your first trip to check out your new room should include cleaning supplies and paper towels. Before you bring in any of your belongings, give everything a good spray and wipe-down with your favorite cleaner. As you and your family carry in your stuff, get to work setting everything up before your parents and helpers leave.

> **Note**
>
> Make sure to take a visit to the bookstore to purchase your textbooks and supplies before your parents leave. Even if they aren't buying, it's great to have a ride back to your dorm with your purchases. All those books are heavy! Also, remember to bring your class schedule so you know which textbooks to buy.

You can't live without your laptop, phone, iPad, iPod, or other technological devices, and the good news is that all of these items will be quite useful and necessary while you're away at college. Remember to pack a few surge protectors/power strips, all charging cords, and locks or lockboxes to secure all equipment and valuables while you're away from your room.

Other necessary key equipment includes a desk or clip-on lamp, a backpack/book bag, an umbrella, and athletic equipment (tennis racket, baseball mitt). Please remember that most colleges prohibit extension cords, halogen lights, candles, incense, and air conditioners.

Bed Bath & Beyond offers great products, services, and resources for college students under the Shop for College tab on their website at www.bedbathandbeyond.com. It includes a college gift registry, decorating ideas, and a shopping guide and checklist.

Do your best to prepare, but remember that you aren't traveling to Mars. There's bound to be a Target, Walmart, or other all-purpose store nearby—and if not, you'll survive until your parents can mail it to you in a care package.

Greek Life

Greek life refers to membership in either a fraternity (male) or sorority (female) community. Some colleges rely heavily on Greek life for social structure and opportunities, which include parties, community-service events, and formal affairs. Other schools have few Greek organizations on and near campus, while some offer no opportunities for students to participate.

Fraternities and sororities are named by a combination of two or three Greek letters. Often, the Greek letters are shortened to a contracted version. Greek Rank at www.GreekRank.com lists the largest Greek organizations in the U.S. by school chapters.[1]

Fraternities

Name	Greek Letters	Nickname
Tau Kappa Epsilon	ΤΚΕ	Teke
Sigma Phi Epsilon	ΣΦΕ	SigEp
Kappa Sigma	ΚΣ	KS-Kappa Sig
Sigma Alpha Epsilon	ΣΑΕ	SAE-Sigma Alpha Epsilon
Sigma Chi	ΣΧ	Sig Chi-Sigma Chis

Sororities

Name	Greek Letters	Nickname
Chi Omega	ΧΩ	Chi O
Delta Zeta	ΔΖ	DZ
Alpha Phi	ΑΦ	AP
Zeta Tau Alpha	ΖΤΑ	Zetas
Delta Gamma	ΔΓ	DG

Rush is the designated period of time when prospective members are introduced to each and every organization (fraternities for men, sororities for women) and their members at sponsored social events. During this time, *Rushees* are courted for membership while exposed to the mission and culture of each organization.

---

[1] Information from www.greekrank.com/rankings/size/.

Bids are invitations to join the organization. A bid is usually a formal, written invite, which may be delivered to a Rushee with fanfare and ceremony. Some students may receive multiple bids or invites; however, a Rushee may only accept the bid from one organization. In a disappointing situation, a Rushee may not receive a bid from his or her favorite organization—or any, for that matter.

Once Rushees accepts their bids, they are considered *Pledges* who are allowed to wear the "letters" of the organization with their pledge pins. With this honor, Pledges endure a time period when they are "pledging" allegiance to the organization.

After successfully completing this often-tiring experience, Pledges participate in an initiation ceremony, where they are ultimately accepted as full-fledged members of the organization. These new members, called *Brothers* or *Sisters*, look forward to the opportunity to woo next year's Rushees and initiate the Pledges.

It is a personal decision to join a fraternity or sorority. The character and importance of Greek life is different at each college. Most students choose membership because fraternities and sororities offer wonderful opportunities for lifelong friendships and affiliation, charitable endeavors, and leadership opportunities.

Finding a roommate is always something that a lot of people worry about. While visiting a school, try to find out who else is looking at the school. Regardless, you're going to have to take a risk living with someone while at college, and the experience is five times more valuable than if you lived by yourself.

—Andrew H., Towson University, Maryland

Chapter 15
Topics to Contemplate

Go Greek. It was one of the best experiences and decisions of my life. Just get to know all the fraternities and sororities and see if you fit in. I never thought I would go Greek, but after going out a lot and meeting brothers and partying, I knew it was for me.

—Steve C., York College of Pennsylvania

Throughout life, knowledge and awareness of issues are your best defenses against potential hazards. Don't be disturbed by these topics, just be prepared and ready to take action if and when necessary. Read through the brief descriptions and consider each while judging or assessing your reaction and attitudes toward it. Follow up on those topics that concern you and your parents the most.

Senioritis

According to UrbanDictionary.com, "Senioritis is a crippling disease that strikes high school seniors. Symptoms include laziness and an over-excessive wearing of track pants, old athletic shirts, sweatpants, athletic shorts, and sweatshirts. Other features include a lack of studying, repeated absences, and a generally dismissive attitude. The only known cure is a phenomenon known as graduation."

High school seniors believe they deserve a break. You've studied, been tested, performed community service, completed applications, visited colleges, and been accepted. You think you're tired and worn out, but you're not really. Life is just starting to become interesting, and this is no time to rest.

However, some seniors check out by sleeping through classes, missing assignments, not studying, and not caring. They think they have it all figured out because they've been accepted to college, but they should read the fine print. Your college has the right to *rescind* (take back) their offer of acceptance at any time. So if your grades fall, you fail a course, or you are involved in disciplinary or legal troubles, be prepared. You may have to make alternate plans.

Point to Ponder

You're about to attend college with all smart kids, like yourself, with the same credentials. You're going to read a lot, study, and take tests, all while adapting to new rules and a new environment and making new friends. Is this a good time to disconnect from learning? Are you becoming a lazy-bones? Is it too much to sit and concentrate in school when you think you have better things to do? Are you starting to blow off your responsibilities? When will you stop?

End the school year strong and maintain (if not improve) your senior year grades. Positively contribute to your classes and enjoy spending time with your high school friends and teachers. Meet and exceed expectations!

Make good choices. Remember, you are not in college until you move into your dorm. Keep out of trouble and don't fail any courses your senior year. Colleges have the option of rescinding admission offers. Also, under new federal financial-aid guidelines, all students must verify that they are high school graduates by the first week of July in order to qualify for financial aid, so make sure you don't have to go to summer school your senior year.

—Emmanuel Cruz, Admissions Counselor, Hartwick College, New York

Learning Styles

Take a moment to think about how you learn best. In high school, teachers work very hard to adapt to all styles and levels of learners. Lessons include visual (seeing), auditory (hearing), and kinesthetic (hands-on) methods and activities, geared to reach all students. The focus is student-centered, with teachers accountable to students, parents, and school administrators.

Point to Ponder

In high school, students experience varying degrees of success. Students earn 70s or C's, 80s or B's, and 90s or A's for their averages and are each accepted to certain caliber colleges. So, if you are an A student, expect to attend college with mostly A students. Be prepared to learn and compete with students just like you. Watch out: You may not be the smartest kid in class anymore.

In college, professors teach using *their* own preferred methodology, with lecture being the most popular. You need to identify each of your professors' teaching styles and adapt it to your own learning style in order to succeed. It is a skill that usually takes a semester or two to master.

- Visual learners do well reading textbooks and studying notes. They do not find study groups productive, but rather prefer to study alone.

- Auditory learners succeed by listening to live and taped lectures and discussing study topics with others.

- Kinesthetic learners excel at actions and processes that they can repeat and master. It's all about hands-on learning.

 If you're not sure about your preferred style, take the VARK Assessment questionnaire designed by Neil Fleming, at www.vark-learn.com. The VARK Guide to Learning Styles includes help sheets to assist visual, aural, read/write, kinesthetic, and multimodal learners in supporting and adapting their personal learning styles.

Naviance offers a Learning Style inventory to help identify conditions that support your efforts to study efficiently and effectively. Do you like bright lights or dim? Are snacks necessary? Does listening to music allow you to remember and learn better? Do you even know what you like? It's time to find out, because college is expensive, and you need to maintain high grades to receive the best financial aid and career opportunities.

Binge Drinking

Binge drinking is the most common type of drinking done on college campuses today. Do you think college students open a bottle of wine to have a glass after dinner while reading the paper? Not quite. Students are working hard, studying conscientiously most days to prepare for the upcoming week's assignments and exams. However, on Friday and Saturday nights, and perhaps one weekday night as well, many students are partying hard, letting off some steam by engaging in heavy drinking.

According to the National Institute on Alcohol Abuse and Alcoholism at www.niaaa.nih.gov/alcohol-health/overview-alcohol-consumption/moderate-binge-drinking, "Binge drinking means drinking so much within about 2 hours that blood alcohol concentration (BAC) levels reach 0.08g/dL. For women, this usually happens after about 4 drinks, and for men, after about 5."

This type of drinking can pose health and safety risks, and over the long term can damage the liver and other organs. Whether it is a social function, a house party, a formal event, a fraternity party, a night out at the bar, or a tailgate, it's all about binge drinking.

There are countless statistics and terribly tragic tales about accidents and deaths that were the result of poor judgment due to binge drinking.

Alcohol poisoning, which can result in brain damage and death, the harshest effect of binge drinking, occurs when relatively large amounts of alcohol are ingested in a comparatively short amount of time. This doesn't necessarily mean drinking a bottle of liquor over the course of a night, but it may. It could be a result of drinking multiple shots of alcohol in an hour or two by someone who has an empty stomach, is on a prescription medication, or has a low weight.

How does it happen? Well, most have witnessed it at one time or another. People are out partying, having a great time. Someone appears to have been over-served, drinking too much. That person slurs his or her words, is tired, and wants to go to sleep— or just wavers, falls down, and passes out.

What happens next? Friends may put the person in the shower, feed him or her cups of coffee, or just put the drinker to bed. Others may see this as a medical emergency, call an ambulance, and summon medical care.

It is impossible to determine the right thing to do. There is no absolute formula for alcohol poisoning, and there is no way to know when someone's life is at risk, because it is all happening internally. Victims' friends swear that if they knew the drinker was in distress and needed medical attention, they would've acted immediately, no matter the consequences, but alcohol poisoning is a silent killer.

Red Watch Band at www.stonybrook.edu/sb/redwatchband is an organization that promotes awareness of the dangers of toxic drinking, sponsors training sessions for college students to identify warning signs, and provides emergency response.

Additionally, all colleges sponsor in-house training sessions to students, via residence-hall education programs relating to student safety, including alcohol- and drug-use awareness and prevention.

AlcoholEdu for College at college.alcoholedu.com is a web-based awareness and prevention program required by some colleges. Students enter the site with their assigned user names and passwords, and college administrators are notified of program completion.

Date Rape

Date or acquaintance rape is a prevalent form of sexual assault on college campuses today. The combination of young men and women under the influence of alcohol and/or drugs may lead to impaired judgment with potentially disastrous consequences for all parties involved.

> **Scenario**
>
> Two students who know each other socially and enjoy each other's company meet up at a late-night party where alcohol is available and has been heavily consumed. The two walk home and end up in the same room, where they begin an intimate encounter. Upon waking or becoming sober, one student determines that she did not give consent, which leaves both parties in an awkward and vulnerable state. One student feels she has been taken advantage of, victimized, and potentially assaulted. The other is accused and judged. Whether or not law enforcement is called and an investigation with criminal charges proceeds, neither student is unharmed, with both feeling humiliated, violated, and burdened.

If you plan to engage in any type of romantic behavior, be sober and consenting. If you feel mature enough to participate, then do so without drinking alcohol, which many use to decrease inhibitions.

Certain chemicals, called *date-rape drugs*, are used to take advantage of unsuspecting victims when they are added to beverages, according to Women'sHealth.gov at www.womenshealth.gov/publications/our-publications/fact-sheet/date-rape-drugs.cfm. Never leave your glass unattended, accept open drinks from strangers, or consume from punchbowls or larger containers, as these are prone to tampering.

The commonly used date-rape drugs are Rohypnol (roofies), GHB (Gamma 10), Ketamine (Special K), and MDMA (Ecstasy); these can induce memory loss and uninhibited behavior. Recently, large numbers of party attendees have required medical attention and hospitalization due to drug-drink tampering.

The buddy system is appropriate when traveling to and participating in social functions or events. Use and respect it, regardless of whether alcohol is consumed. Never leave a (wo)man behind. If alcohol is consumed, judgment is impaired. Because your friend may not have the sense to leave if he or she is having too much fun, if required, pressure everyone to leave the party together and arrive home safely.

Drug Use

Drug use is a crime. I'm not going to debate the merits or dangers. Some students choose to participate in recreational drug use, which presents the same dangers as binge drinking, with the additional kicker of arrest and jail time.

Hazing

According to StopHazing at www.stophazing.org, "Hazing refers to any activity expected of someone joining a group (or to maintain full status in a group) that humiliates, degrades or risks emotional and/or physical harm, regardless of the person's willingness to participate." Hazing is illegal but has been commonplace among athletic teams, instrumental bands, fraternities and sororities, and other groups. There have been instances of hazing that resulted in hospitalization and death, with criminal charges filed against the perpetrators.

Colleges and universities have taken steps to prevent hazing, creating no-tolerance policies. Organizations have been disbanded and barred from campus for allegations of hazing. Expect to receive training in hazing awareness and prevention and to be asked to sign documents stating that you will not allow yourself to be hazed or participate in hazing activities.

However, hazing is often deemed as tradition. The behavior is passed down from one generation to the next, often expressed as, "I had to endure this, and now I'm going to do the same to someone else." Consider it a cycle of abuse.

Not all organizations participate in hazing activities. However, according to student feedback and news reports, it still *does* exist, so be aware. Make smart choices. Don't put yourself in danger or harm's way, and watch out for your friends as well.

> *Look into all of the clubs, sororities, and fraternities at the school you go to. Anybody can join, just be aware. Hazing is illegal, but it doesn't mean people don't do it.*
>
> **—Jessica F., Seton Hall University, New Jersey**

Health and Wellness

Be mindful of your own health and wellness while in college. There are many opportunities for poor nutrition and lack of sleep, combined with the stress and pressures of classes, exams, and assignments.

Eat well, and that means making healthy choices. Get enough sleep; you know how it feels to be tired or exhausted. When you don't feel well, go to the Health Center or see a doctor. Also, keep your parents apprised of your condition. Your well being is their number-one concern.

Keep physically fit by exercising. Colleges have fitness facilities and opportunities for physical activities, including intramural and team sports. Some public and private colleges require credits for physical education classes, including tennis, golf, swimming, volleyball, badminton, and others. Regardless of whether it is required, stay active!

If you feel sad, depressed, or stressed, seek out assistance. Colleges offer amazing programs just for you, and you aren't the only one. Reach out to your network of support and be available to others in their time of need. Keep your parents up to date on your progress, experiences, and attitude toward school.

Academic Integrity

You shouldn't cheat, and you've known this for a long time. In high school, if you got caught, the repercussions were minor—a call home, a zero on a quiz, or detention. In college, cheating or academic dishonesty is taken very seriously, and so are the consequences.

 Colleges support academic integrity for their students and staff by incorporating specific principles into their codes of conduct. Failure to adhere to and abide by these principles jeopardizes the college's reputation and the student's status. Use the search box on your college's official website to locate its academic dishonesty and/or academic integrity policies.

> **Caution**
>
> Often, students accused of academic dishonesty are charged with not properly citing or giving credit for others' works, words, and ideas. Be familiar with the requirements of each of your professors. The required citation styles include APA (for psychology, education, and other social sciences), MLA (for literature, arts, and humanities), AMA (for medicine, health, and biological sciences), and Turabian and Chicago Manual of Style (for all subjects).

Examples of violations include plagiarism, cheating, fabrication, facilitating dishonesty, and academic sabotage. Examples of punishments or sanctions include dismissal, course failure, disciplinary probation, suspension, or permanent expulsion.

> *Stay out of trouble. I don't know how other schools work, but at my school the RA's (residential assistants) walk through every hall from about 10:30 p.m. until the early hours of the morning. If your room is making too much noise, they will knock on your door and ask you to be quiet. However, if they smell or see anything that you shouldn't have in your room, you will be put on probation and letters will be sent home to your parents. Once you are put on probation at my school, you're on probation until the day you graduate. You can still have fun at college; you just need to be smart about it.*
>
> **—Lauren H., SUNY Albany, New York**

Citation makers by EasyBib at www.easybib.com and RefWorks at www.refworks.com are two of the many Internet-based reference guides and management software tools available to assist you in meeting the requirements of your school's academic integrity policy. Also, your college's academic services center may assist you with proofreading and editorial support.

Turnitin at www.TurnItIn.com is an Internet-based program that "detects unoriginal content in students' written work." Some professors will instruct you to log in and upload assignments as part of the submission requirements. Be aware that modern technology can be used to hold you accountable for your own work.

> *To be honest, the hardest part of the transition was getting used to their style of how things get done here. I am just recently starting to mature and get out of "summer mode." College is no joke. It is impossible to just sit in class and listen to professors and hope that you will be fine for the next quiz/exam. I have already learned this the hard way.*
>
> **—Richie O., Siena College, New York**

> *If you are not annotating or hate doing it, learn to do it and learn to love it. I have to read about 50+ pages of material almost every single night for all of my classes combined (and so does everyone else), and if I didn't know how to annotate coming into college, I would probably be screwed, to say the least!*
>
> **—Carli C., Quinnipiac University, Connecticut**

> *It's so annoying that everything is emailed to you, rather than told to you in class. Most teachers just end class by telling you to "review the syllabus," and then it is your responsibility to find out whether or not you have an assignment due.*
>
> **—Richie O., Siena College, New York**

PART VIII
How It Plays Out

"College is the best time of your life." You've heard it a thousand times. Hopefully it's true. (I prefer to believe that life keeps getting better and better with each stage, but I'm a lot older than you.) Even if it's not exactly like *Animal House*, *Back to School*, *Old School*, or any other college-life movie, you are sure to gain an extensive library of memories and photos to share. Warning: Watch out for those cell-phone photos and videos—they can catch you in some compromising situations that you may hope to forget. Remember, the Internet is forever!

However, some college students are hounded by strained relationships, homesick-ness, frustrating progress (or lack thereof), and general dissatisfaction. It's nothing like they thought it was going to be, for any number of possible reasons. Some choose to go home, transfer out, or discontinue their studies altogether. Again, I prefer to take the most positive viewpoint and approach to college, with curiosity, character, and optimism. Go get 'em!

Chapter 16
This Is Awesome!

Get involved. I am currently in the ping-pong club, volleyball club, student government, the poker club, and the Formula 1 race team. Also, I am on three different intramural volleyball teams. Stay active and have fun!

—Ryan S., Florida Institute of Technology, Florida

Have high expectations for personal growth, fun, and success in college. It's a great time in your life, and it goes by fast. Ask people you know about their college years, and they will reflect on them with a far-off look in their eyes and a mysterious smile on their face.

For Students

The first few weeks of school are a whirlwind of activities, classes, and new friends. The feelings are overwhelming. They are part shock, part freedom, and part fear. Some students adapt to the new environment very well, and others struggle with the transition. There are good days and bad days during this process. Even students who love college have moments of sadness and homesickness. It is normal.

During your first few days at school, be a keen observer. Take time to absorb and reflect on the people you meet, the activities available, and the campus in general. You have the power to start off on the right foot. For many, this will be the time to shed the expectations of others and social pressures and history from high school. Repackage your sparkling personality, but be true to yourself. You now have a fresh audience for all of your jokes, advice, and laughs. Enjoy making new friends!

Having too much fun is a definite possibility at college, but you need to remember why you're there: to get an education and prepare for a successful career. Your experience at orientation can be deceiving. It feels like day camp for 18-year-olds with its activities, games, and barbecues, especially since classes aren't in session. Once classes begin, you need to settle in and focus.

Social life is a great time anywhere you go—some schools more than others—but it is what you make of it.

—Andrew H., Towson University, Maryland

Some students have so much fun and adapt so well to the college social scene that they blow off their academic responsibilities. They skip classes, do poorly on exams, and miss assignments. For those students, the fun comes to a crashing halt pretty quickly. Either college administrators will send them home permanently due to poor performance or their own parents will pull them out for wasting time and money.

> **Cautionary Tale**
>
> At college, I partied the whole time. I rarely went to class. It was a blast. By the end of my freshman year, I had only passed three classes. I had to leave. Now I have $15,000 worth of loans to pay back for nothing.
>
> —Anonymous

Ups and downs are also part of the college experience. There're semesters where your course load is especially challenging and stressful, while other semesters are a breeze. There are times when your social calendar is full, and others when you feel a bit lonely. Relationships can also influence your experience at school, whether you are in a positive, healthy relationship or you're embroiled in drama. For better or worse, heartache, breakups, new love, and reconciliations are all part of the mix.

My roommate and I get along really well even though we are very different. It is definitely better to room with someone who is somewhat different from you because if you are with someone who is too much like you for a long amount of time, it gets to be too much (especially if you have the opportunity to pick your own roommates!). We did not have the chance to pick our own roommates; the university does random selection based on a survey that you must complete.

—**Carli C., Quinnipiac University, Connecticut**

For Parents

"They never call" is a phrase commonly spoken by parents of college-age children. You can take it as a good sign that they are wrapped up in their studies, socializing, fulfilling obligations, and assuming responsibility. Even so, it is still your job to set high expectations for your student while in school. No matter who pays the bills, it's important for students to know that they will not be permitted to "party on" at college if their overall grades are unsatisfactory.

Parents' weekend is a great opportunity to see your student as a member of the college community. Usually centered on a fall football game or sporting event, you'll have the opportunity to meet your student's friends and their parents. You and your student can walk around campus, attend events, and interact in a new way. Let your student show *you* around and explain to *you* how things work and what they do.

Use this time to assess your student's progress, social adjustment, and satisfaction with college by asking many questions and being an attentive listener.

First-semester grades can be a disappointing topic. As previously mentioned, growth and transitions happen during this first semester. Students living on campus must adapt to being away from family, sharing a room, managing meals, and making new friends. Those commuting to college must navigate traffic, parking, and weather conditions while having to really reach out to others in class to make new friends. Don't forget the new learning environment that requires them to sit in class for an hour, read many pages of college-level text each night, and sit and focus in lectures of up to 200 students.

Considering all of these factors, expect your student to struggle on the first two or three exams. Students arrive confident that the effort and study habits that helped them excel in high school will be enough to get them through college. Most often, it's not the case. The first exam grade is enough to get them into gear, and that's when the learning curve kicks in. Students quickly realize that they must adapt here as well.

Expect your student to seek out help if and when it's needed. Many academic support services and tutors are available to assist students with challenging coursework. Set a standard for proactive behavior. If your student receives a D or an F on the first exam, with effort, hard work, and determination, there may still be the potential to earn a B in the course.

Support and expect your student to extend himself by reaching out to professors during their office hours. In addition to communicating with professors, expect your student to keep you updated with quick progress reports and check-ins.

> **Cautionary Tale**
>
> According to the numbers, I had an 89.1 average in my criminal justice class. I really wanted an A, and I was so close. I figured I'd give it a try, so I went to my professor's office hours to ask for an extra point. You know what? He remembered me coming to get extra help at different times throughout the semester. It paid off. I got my A.
>
> —Darrin P., University of Delaware

All is not lost if the first year is transitional. Students who struggle initially often experience huge personal growth, and they begin to take responsibility for their learning and academic progress. They start to really understand the system, professors' expectations and yours, and the costs of attending college.

> *Put yourself out there the first week, introduce yourself to everyone, and make friends. My roommate did not do this; I did. I went to every welcome-weekend activity, and they were useful and fun. The best part is that I met the people I now hang out with.*
>
> —**Leanne S., Hartwick College, New York**

The social aspect of school is really good. You would be amazed at how many friends you make in the first two weeks of school and classes.

—Patrick F., SUNY Cortland, New York

When I finish this class next week, I will have the biggest grin on my face, knowing that despite that 15-page research paper that took me four months to do properly, I've grown a lot of patience and determination.

—Katherine N., Suffolk County Community College, New York

Chapter 17
I Hate It Here

Be yourself, because when people try to re-create themselves at a college, they tend not to stay there. Homesickness happens, but if you just make a nice group of friends at school, it can be a second family.

—Jessica F., Seton Hall University, New Jersey

It's not always a shock when students don't like being away at college. Even commuter students may experience a sense of disappointment. Often these thoughts and feelings are just temporary, part of the transition, but sometimes they may indicate real distress. Parents and students must communicate and work to identify issues, determining the causes and necessary solutions together. You and your parents should contemplate these common concerns to easily recognize them, prevent them or resolve them in the future.

For Students

Moving on in life is exciting, but it can often be overwhelming, too. Leaving your best friends, family, and home can upset the very foundation of your life. You're basically on your own, one step closer to being an independent adult. You may feel alone at first, but these insecurities allow for personal growth, where you'll ultimately learn that you're capable and strong.

Don't be too hard on yourself. Accept moments of weakness. Keep moving forward. The poem "Desiderata" by Max Ehrmann provides great inspiration and quality life-advice. It is a personal favorite that has guided many through challenging times.

Homesickness affects all students, but at different intensities and times. It may occur during the first few days of school, or it can develop after a month or so, when the initial excitement wears off a bit. Often it happens a year or two into college, when one is facing a difficult situation.

Challenging, college-level assignments can cause you to become overwhelmed by your responsibilities. When stress and the workload increase, you may yearn for the simplicity and ease of high school. Some students are in over their heads when it comes to meeting the demands of college. Take into account that you were accepted into college because you met the standards. All you need to do is adjust your habits and make a commitment to achieve success, whatever it takes. Don't put too much pressure on yourself by expecting to get a 4.0 just because you did in high school. You can do well, so do it!

Commuter students often complain that college life isn't much different for them. The learning environment is similar to what they experienced in high school—sitting quietly, taking notes, and listening to the professor. Living at home means abiding by parents' rules and helping out around the house. There are no wild fraternity parties, and most students spend their extra hours working part time. The social scene can be limiting because many high school friends are away at school. It takes real effort to immerse yourself in college activities as a commuter student. You can accomplish it by spending extra time on campus, joining clubs, and putting yourself out there to make new friends.

Roommate and housing issues are enough to break any person. Your dorm room is the one place that should offer safety and security while you're away from home. If you and your roommate(s) aren't on good terms or if you're finding it difficult to transition to the college lifestyle, the stress will permeate all other areas of your experience. Your resident assistant (RA) and residence-life office staff are there to help facilitate and mediate any issues. Keep them updated of any difficulties you and your roommate(s) are experiencing. This is their area of expertise, and they can make reassignments if necessary.

Reach out to your network of support, for any and all reasons. Speak with your parents and family, friends from home and nearby schools, college staff and professors, and new classmates. I guarantee that each one has been in challenging life situations before and can give a world-class pep talk when asked.

If you would like to come home for a weekend, plan a visit. Check carpool opportunities and mass-transit schedules, but try not to miss any classes. Sometimes you just need a break from the rat race to gain perspective. When you return to school, you'll have a new outlook and a restored spirit.

"I'm done." It's been said before. If your situation is intolerable and you're at the end of your rope, reach out and call your parents. If you've been talking to them frequently, they probably won't be too surprised. For some, going away to college sounds great in theory but not in reality. You still have potential to do great things. You may go away to college again in the future, if you'd like. Remember that there are always great options for college close to home. Just breathe.

> **Cautionary Tale**
>
> I lasted six weeks at college. I was really excited to go, but living there was impossible. There were overcrowded bathroom facilities and a limited dining-hall schedule that didn't allow me to have my basic needs met. It just wasn't working. So I withdrew and went home. The next semester I enrolled at community college and went on to earn my degree.
>
> —Amy W., Nassau Community College alumna, New York

For Parents

Homesickness can tear at a parent's heart. You want your student to thrive during this new stage of life, not to be tearful, sad, or regretful of the choices he or she made. Your first inclination may be to jump in the car, get there, and fix the problem. It may just be the transition or a temporary experience, although it may be difficult to determine. Yes, your leisurely weekend visit at college is always appreciated, when your student gets to see friendly faces and enjoy some comforts of home away from home.

Keep in mind that difficulties and challenges are always around the corner. Help your child to build "strength of spirit" skills to help him or her throughout life. Speak with your student frequently, be a good listener, and ask questions. Communication is the key.

"I'm done." It happens. Some students leave school to come home after two days, six weeks, or the first semester. Parents must take the trip back to school, pack up, and come home to decide what to do next. This is a setback, but be proud that your student gave it a try. At least your student was willing to put himself or herself out there to experience life at college. It is not for every kid. Help your son or daughter get back on track by contacting his or her high school guidance counselor and developing a new plan. He or she will know exactly what to do; your student isn't the first.

A *reverse transfer* occurs when a student begins college away at a four-year institution but then leaves to come home and attend a two-year community school. This option is feasible for many students as a result of poor grades, changing financial conditions, or personal reasons.

Point to Ponder

By the end of freshman year, it's usually apparent which students plan to and deserve to return to school. If your student is accumulating debt and at the same time not earning credits toward his or her degree, it may be time to discuss or demand a change.

If you have roommate problems, realize it isn't the end of the world. You don't have to like the person; you just have to live with them. Treat them with respect, and you should be fine. Be reasonable, and if there ever is a problem, go to an RA; they can tell you how to handle it.

—**Leanne S., Hartwick College, New York**

My roommate freshman year was terrible. I moved off campus with eight of my closest friends for this year.

—Mike H., Boston University, Massachusetts

It's not for everyone. Not everyone needs a college degree; however, everyone deserves the opportunity to give it a chance. Some students are born entrepreneurs, others do well in trade occupations, and some thrive in the military. Success has many paths.

Appendix A
Glossary of Key Terms

academic advisor. Staff member or professor who assists you in course registration and college and career guidance.

academic dishonesty policy. Outline of offenses and punishments related to cheating and plagiarism.

academic index. Three criteria used to rate and evaluate applicants in college admissions process, which include GPA, college admissions exam scores, and course/curriculum rigor.

academic integrity. Honesty and responsibility in education.

academic probation. Notification of poor academic performance, which may lead to expulsion from school.

accepted. You have met the criteria for entrance to the school. However, the offer may be rescinded due to declining grades or disciplinary issues.

ACCUPLACER at http://www.collegeboard.com/student/testing/accuplacer/. Commonly used, computerized placement tests.

ACT at www.actstudent.org. Formerly known as American College Test. College entrance/admissions exam. Consists of five areas of assessment: English, reading, math, science, and writing. Top composite score of 36.

activity sheet/resume. Comprehensive log of extracurricular activities, listing names, dates, statistics, and brief descriptions. Includes honors, community-service projects, and awards.

admissions office counselor/officer/advisor. College staff who promote programs to prospective students and parents. Usually responsible for specific territories or states. May also participate in admissions decisions individually or by committee.

admissions office/undergraduate. Staff dedicated to providing admission services to incoming freshman and undergraduate transfer students.

Advanced Placement (AP) courses/exams. Higher-level courses and exams used to advance knowledge and application, offered in 34 courses. Students may earn credits for college based on exam scores. Administered by College Board.

alcohol poisoning. Sickness or death caused by excessive alcohol intake.

AlcoholEdu for College at www.college.alcoholedu.com. Prevention and awareness program often required for college freshman.

alma mater. The school, university, or college that one attended.

application. Data forms used to evaluate prospective students.

associate's degree. Earned by completing course requirements of approximately 63 credits, usually in two years.

bachelor's degree. Earned by completing course requirements of approximately 126 credits, usually in four years.

bid. Invitation, usually formal and written, to join a fraternity or sorority.

binge drinking. Ingesting many alcoholic beverages within a limited period of time.

Blue Light emergency phone system. Campus safety feature that connects users directly with campus police.

campus visit. Opportunity to explore college grounds and facilities. May include a formal tour or open-house event. Best scheduled when students are on campus and attending classes.

Career Interest Profiler (Naviance). Assessment used to determine career interests, provided by Naviance web-based software.

CEEB code. Identification numbers assigned to high schools, colleges, and other programs by College Board. These are needed during the college application process.

citations. Reference to the source of another's work. Varies in style, including MLA, APA, and Chicago.

Cluster Finder (Naviance). Assessment used to determine broad areas of career interest, provided by Naviance web-based software.

co-op/cooperative program. Valuable, real-world work experience completed as part of a school's academic program and/or requirements.

college applications. Forms, usually completed online, that allow college admissions staff to evaluate prospective students.

College Board at www.collegeboard.org. Non-profit organization responsible for administering education testing, including PSAT, SAT, and SAT subject tests, and other educational services.

College Board's Book of Majors. Soft-cover resource that lists and describes hundreds of programs of study and career outcomes.

college entrance exam/college admissions exam. Assessments used to evaluate prospective students, usually SAT or ACT.

college essay. 200- to 500-word original work written by applicants. Used by college staff to evaluate prospective students.

college fair. National, regional, and local forums where college admissions representatives provide information and brochures to prospective students and parents.

College Navigator at http://nces.ed.gov/collegenavigator/. Internet database and resource used to research college and program information and statistics.

college visits (Naviance). Information sessions held at high schools where college admissions staff present to prospective students in a small group setting.

Common Application at www.commonapp.org. Web portal that allows students to apply to many colleges using universal application forms and requirements.

commuter students. Students who drive or take mass transit to classes each day. Non-residential students.

conditional acceptance. You are offered admission to the school on the condition that you complete/fulfill additional requirements.

cost of attendance. Total money needed to attend school for one year, including additional expenses.

credits/credit hours. Units earned by successfully completing a course. Determined by weekly class duration.

CSS/Financial Aid PROFILE at https://profileonline.collegeboard.org. Additional financial-aid information required by select colleges before the application deadline. Administered by College Board.

date rape/acquaintance rape. Sexual assault or attempted sexual assault perpetrated by a known or familiar person. Prevalent on college campuses due to alcohol use and lack of supervision.

date-rape drugs. Chemicals added to drinks that induce memory-loss and/or uninhibited behaviors.

deadline. Stated date, most often strictly adhered to.

declaring a major. Process of committing to a specific program of study. Usually required by first semester of junior year of college.

deferred. (1) Your early-action/early-decision application has been reassigned to the regular admission pool for further consideration. (2) Your regular admissions decision has been postponed pending additional information. (3) You have been accepted for enrollment for the spring semester.

doctoral degree. Professional degree earned by completing graduate school, usually more than 60 credits.

early action/non-restrictive early action. Opportunity to submit application materials by an earlier deadline with the expectation of receiving an admission decision more quickly.

early decision. Legally binding opportunity to commit *to one college* during application process. Upon acceptance, student pledges to withdraw all other applications. Requires an early application deadline.

early release. Opportunity for high school students to leave school early each day by not registering for or needing a full schedule of classes.

electronic calendar. Digital calendar or time-management tool, usually web-based.

email account. Commonly used as user ID for Internet portals. May be used for communication with admission staff.

Expected Family Contribution (EFC). Measure of your family's financial position, which is used by schools to determine federal student aid. Calculated using numbers entered on the FAFSA.

extra-long, twin mattress. Common size of bedding required for college residence halls/dorm rooms.

extracurricular activities. Participation in clubs, groups, sports teams, or organizations.

FAFSA4caster at https://fafsa.ed.gov or https://fafsa.ed.gov/FAFSA/app/f4cForm? execution=e1s1. U. S. Department of Education's website tool used to determine eligibility and estimates for federal student aid.

Family Connection by Naviance. Internet portal used by parents and students to access Naviance subscription software. Website links vary by high school. Speak with your guidance counselor for registration code and instructions.

Family Education and Rights Privacy Act (FERPA) waiver. Signed document that determines specific rights of privacy for student academic and financial records.

FastWeb at www.fastweb.com. Searchable Internet database of available scholarships and grants.

federal school codes. Used to identify schools when applying for financial aid through the FAFSA.

Federal Student Aid at www.studentaid.ed.gov. Largest source of aid, funded through the U. S. Department of Education, includes loans, grants, and work-study programs.

fee waivers. Financial assistance for college entrance exams and application fees. Available to students experiencing financial hardship.

FinAid at www.FinAid.org. Private web-based resource for financial-aid support and information.

financial-aid award letter. Summary of financial-aid components, including grants, loans, and scholarships offered by each school.

financial/student aid. Financial assistance in the form of grants, scholarships, loans, and work study, used to pay for college.

fraternities. Social organization, designated by Greek letters, traditionally for men.

Free Application for Federal Student Aid (FAFSA) at www.fafsa.ed.gov. Secure Internet portal used to submit financial data to U. S. Department of Education. This data is then used to determine student aid eligibility.

government student loans. Financial-aid program administered by the U. S. Department of Education that includes subsidized and unsubsidized loans that must be repaid.

grace period. Length of time, regarding a student loan, when you do not have to make payments. Typically six months after graduation or after part-time enrollment.

grade-point average (GPA). In *college*, weighted calculation of cumulative average determined by final course grades and credit hours, traditionally on a 4.0 scale. A= 4.0, B=3.0, C=2.0, D=1.0. In *high school*, weighted or non-weighted cumulative average determined by final course grades and honors, AP, college-level, IB weighting, if applicable. Either on a 4.0, 5.0, or 100-point scale.

graduate school. Educational programs available after earning bachelor's degree, leading to a professional degree (master's or doctorate).

graduate student. Person enrolled in a professional program or graduate school leading to an advanced degree beyond a bachelor's degree.

graduation rate. Percentage of students who complete their program/degree within a specific period of time, usually 150%.

grants. Aid for students who demonstrate financial need that is considered gift aid because it does not need to be repaid.

Greek life. Available infrastructure and opportunities to join fraternities and sororities.

guidance counselor. High school professional available to assist you with career and college planning, as well as personal issues.

hazing. Activities, events, and behaviors required for acceptance into certain groups. Usually humiliating or abusive in nature.

homesickness. Feeling of sadness or low-level depression due to separation from family, friends, or familiar surroundings. Usually temporary in nature.

honors program. Opportunity for high-achieving and motivated students. Usually requires additional admission requirements. Benefits may include small classes, special activities, and priority course registration.

immediate-decision day/onsite registration. Opportunity to meet with college admissions staff to have application materials evaluated and a decision rendered.

International Baccalaureate. Challenging curriculum and coursework offered by IB program high schools. May earn college credits by exam scores/program completion.

Internet portal. Website interface or database accessed by user ID and password.

learning styles. The modality in which you learn best. Includes visual, auditory, and kinesthetic styles.

liberal arts/core requirements. General-education courses traditionally taken during the first two years of college, including communications, math, history, social sciences, natural sciences, and world-languages classes.

local scholarships. Scholarships awarded by nearby community organizations specifically to local students.

major. A concentration of study, usually 5 to 7 courses (15–22 credits) in addition to core program requirements. Usually taken during the third and fourth years of college.

master's degree. Professional degree earned by completing graduate school, usually 36–50 credits.

matriculated student. An accepted student who is enrolled in a degree-granting program.

May 1st/decision deadline. Universal date for students to inform one school of their final college selection by sending in the required deposit.

millennials. Children born during the late 1980s and 1990s who have different attitudes, behaviors, and values toward many aspects of life.

minor. An optional secondary area of study, usually 4 or 5 courses (12–15 credits).

money factor. Choosing a major, college, or career path based solely on the high annual salary expected.

move-in day. Official date when freshman and/or other students may enter college housing facilities.

My Majors at www.mymajors.com. Internet resource to identify career interests and college majors.

NACAC National College Fair at http://www.nacacnet.org/college-fairs/students-parents/Pages/default.aspx. National Association for College Admission Counseling organization that sponsors networking events for students, parents, and admissions counselors.

National Collegiate Athletic Association (NCAA) at www.eligibilitycenter.org. Determines eligibility of student athletes competing in college sports. Also manages and directs divisional sports programs.

Naviance. Subscription web-based guidance management system used to process and monitor college preparation and application processes.

Net Price Calculator. Federally mandated tool, located on colleges' official websites, which determines true cost of attendance.

non-matriculated student. A visiting student or one who is not seeking a degree.

Occupational Outlook Handbook at www.bls.gov/ooh. Internet resource that reports career descriptions and salary and outlook statistics.

office hours. Posted times when professors are present in their offices and are available for conferences and extra help.

Office of Residential Life/Office of University Housing. Department and staff responsible for all aspects of college housing, including roommate assignments.

official score reports. Notification of college admission exam scores, as sent to colleges directly by College Board or the ACT for a fee.

open house. Campus-wide events for prospective students. Includes guided tours and presentations.

orientation. Program where new students are introduced to campus life through activities, icebreakers, and events.

Parent PLUS loans. Federal financial-aid program that lends money to parents of undergraduate students. Money must be repaid.

personal identification number (PIN) at www.pin.ed.gov. Digital signature used on federal websites. Used by parents and students when completing financial-aid forms.

Personality Type (Naviance). Personality assessment using Myers-Briggs Do What You Are system, provided by Naviance web-based software.

placement tests. Assessments used to determine skills and abilities in math, reading comprehension, and writing. May be used for remedial class assignment.

pledge. Student who accepted a bid but first needs to meet certain criteria and obligations before being initiated as a full-fledged member of a fraternity or sorority.

Preliminary Scholastic Aptitude Test (PSAT) at https://bigfuture.collegeboard.org/get-in/testing/an-introduction-to-the-psat-nmsqt. Scaled-down version of the SAT college entrance/admissions exam. Administered by high schools during 10th or 11th grade. Also called National Merit Scholarship Qualifying Test (NMSQT).

private school. Colleges and universities that are self-funded through tuition and endowments.

private student loans. Loans made by a lender, such as a bank, credit union, or school. Usually more expensive than federal loans. Money must be repaid.

prospective students. Students who may plan to apply and ultimately attend a college.

public/state school. Colleges and universities funded by public tax dollars, usually offering reduced tuition rates to state residents.

ranking. Order of highest calculated GPA in comparison to other students. May be weighted or unweighted.

Rate My Professors at www.ratemyprofessors.com. Website where students provide and access feedback on college professors.

reach school. Potential college whose admission criteria are higher than yours.

Red Watch Band. Student-centered group focused on awareness and prevention of toxic drinking.

regular admissions. Opportunity to submit application materials by a stated deadline after which all admission decisions are issued.

rejected. You have not met the criteria for acceptance.

remedial/developmental courses. Required, non-credit courses used to reinforce skills and abilities in math, reading comprehension, and writing.

rescind. College admissions staff can revoke a student's offer of acceptance, usually due to disciplinary action or poor/failing grades.

residency requirement. Proof necessary to be eligible for reduced-rate tuition from public university/college system.

resilience. Vital characteristic that allows you to adapt to and change with current and changing circumstances.

restricted early action. Opportunity to submit application materials *to only one college* by an earlier deadline with the expectation of receiving an admission decision more quickly. Students may apply to other colleges under regular-decision deadlines.

retention rate. Percentage of freshman students who return to study at that school the next year.

reverse transfer. To leave a four-year residential college in order to attend community or junior college as a commuter student.

rolling admissions. Opportunity to submit application materials as soon as possible with the expectation that admission decisions are issued on an ongoing basis.

room and board. Cost of dorm room and meal plan.

roommate match/WebRoomz. Computerized questionnaire used to successfully match preferences and personalities of roommates.

roommates. One, two, or three students who share a common living area.

Rugg's Recommendations on the Colleges at www.ruggsrecommendations.com. Independent digital or paperback resource used to identify colleges with strong programs and reputations in a variety of majors and areas of concentration.

rushee. Student who expresses interest in joining a fraternity or sorority by attending social events.

safety school. Potential college whose admission criteria are lower than yours.

Sallie Mae at www.SallieMae.com. Education finance company that administers student loans and provides a searchable Internet scholarship and grant database.

SAT subject tests/SAT IIs at http://sat.collegeboard.org/about-tests/sat-subject-tests. One-hour tests used to assess mastery in specific subjects, some of which are required by select colleges. Administered by College Board.

scholarship. Monies awarded by colleges, corporations, community groups, etc. to support higher education. Considered "gift" aid and does not need to be repaid.

Scholastic Aptitude Test (SAT) at www.sat.CollegeBoard.org. College entrance/admissions exam administered by College Board. Consists of three areas of assessment: critical reading, math, and writing. Top score of 2400 points.

self-reported grades. Entering data as reported on high school transcript via secure Internet portal, which is used by college admissions staff to evaluate prospective students.

semester. College term, usually 15 weeks in length. Two per school year: fall and spring.

senioritis. General lack of interest and low performance of high school seniors as they approach graduation.

shot-in-the-dark school. Potential college whose admission criteria are much higher than yours.

Social Security number. U. S. government-issued identification number. Commonly used on college applications, but must be secured to avoid potential identity-theft issues.

sororities. Social organization, designated by Greek letters, traditionally for women.

Student Aid Report (SAR). Financial-aid summary of data that was entered on the Free Application for Federal Student Aid (FAFSA). Specifies your Expected Family Contribution (EFC).

study abroad. Opportunity to earn credits while attending classes in a foreign country. Offered during summer, semester, or full-year terms.

subsidized loan. Federal financial-aid program where loan interest payments are paid by the federal government while you are enrolled in school.

summer session. Optional accelerated college term held in June/July, usually four weeks in length.

super score. As a courtesy, admission staff only considers highest scores from each required section when analyzing college entrance exam results.

supplemental application. Required materials in addition to the college application. May include letters of recommendation, essays, short-response answers, and activity sheet/resume.

syllabus. Course outline that may contain specific information about assignments, projects, tests, and deadlines.

target school. Potential college whose admission criteria are in line or equal to yours.

teacher recommendations. Letters written by teachers, coaches, advisors, or professionals attesting to the potential of the applicant. These are used by college admissions staff to evaluate prospective students.

test-optional schools at www.fairtest.org/university/optional. Colleges that do not required standardized college admission exams as part of application materials.

time management. Skills and tools necessary to successfully manage educational requirements while balancing social and work obligations.

total cost of attendance. Funds needed to pay for tuition, room and board, books, and supplies, plus all other necessary expenses.

trimester. College term, usually 10 weeks in length. Three per school year: fall, winter, and spring.

tuition. Cost of attending classes.

Turn It In at www.turnitin.com. Web-based service for teachers/professors to verify authenticity of written assignments. Identifies potential instances of plagiarism and cheating.

two-year college/community college/junior college. Public college offering associate-level and certificate programs to all students. Usually offers open-enrollment policy.

underclassman. Freshman and sophomore students.

undergraduate student. Person enrolled in a school or program leading to an associate's or a bachelor's degree.

university/college fees. Extra costs for supplemental services, including health, computer, and fitness facilities.

unsubsidized loan. Federal financial-aid program where interest accrues (adds up) while you are enrolled in school.

upperclassman. Junior and senior students.

waitlisted. A standby situation where you have neither been rejected nor been offered enrollment yet.

weighted average. Calculating a cumulative average by incorporating additional importance for honors, AP, college-level, and IB classes.

winter session. Optional accelerated college term held in December/January, usually four weeks in length.

work-study program. Financial-aid program that gives students the opportunity to earn money for expenses.

Appendix B
More Feedback and Tips

*Senior year **flies**, so enjoy every single second of it. I would do absolutely anything to relive those days.*

—Carli C., Quinnipiac University, Connecticut

Never take a class before 10 a.m. if you aren't a morning person. I rarely take notes because I find it hard to pay attention and write, but when I do, I just use a pen and notebook.

—Chelsea R., CUNY Community College, New York City

Some important college tips:
1. *Study hard during the semester, rest during break!*
2. *Buy books on Amazon, never at college bookstore. (They're too expensive at the bookstore.)*
3. *Get involved on campus.*
4. *Maintain a part-time job during the semester. (Gas is expensive!)*

—Shaun H., Suffolk County Community College, New York

Learn how to balance social life and schoolwork, because college is totally different from high school.

—Jessica F., Seton Hall University, New Jersey

Have fun! In the beginning it may seem like everything is thrown at you at once, and it is. But by mid-semester, you will learn how to balance school work, a social life, and sleep. If you don't feel like you can find that balance on your own, there are many services provided by the university/college that can help you to learn time-management skills or even provide tutors if you're struggling in your classes.

—Lauren H., SUNY Albany, New York

Everyone is always nervous about getting a "random" for a roommate. I had a random my first semester, and I thought she was going to be a total loser because, according to her Facebook page, she played the cello and called it her boyfriend, she was obsessed with elephants, and she dressed like my grandma. But when I got there, she wasn't this person at all. She left her cello at home, only brought one poster of elephants, and I ended up "shopping" in her wardrobe a lot. We were best friends.

—Lauren H., SUNY Albany, New York

Don't room with people who are from your own town; they aren't what you think they are. And if you have a girlfriend or boyfriend, break up with them before you go to college.

—Ricky B., Florida Institute of Technology, Florida

You're going to have professors that you love and professors that make you want to drop the class. Trust me, I'm finishing up a class right now, and I've been tempted to throw my tape recorder at my professor several times. Don't drop those classes, though. It'll prepare you for the real world. Dealing with people you don't like is the most frustrating yet most rewarding thing.

—Katherine N., Suffolk County Community College, New York

Take this from the Queen of Procrastination herself: DON'T DO IT. I was a procrastinator throughout high school, and eventually you get everything done by the end of the year. In college, you have double the work and half the time to do it. The day you get an assignment is the day you should start it. Don't like that idea? Okay, leave it until the last minute. I'm willing to bet anything that you'll fall asleep during those infamous college all-nighters, or your computer will crash when you're typing up the final paragraph of your term paper. Just get it done. Then when your classmates have bags under their eyes with a coffee in hand, complaining about how the big paper is stressing them out, you know you don't have anything to worry about.

—Katherine N., Suffolk County Community College, New York

If you're someone like me who can't study without music, here's a great tip: Listen to classical music. Don't listen to music with lyrics to it; you'll focus too much on singing along to it. I listen to either symphony orchestras or operas in other languages. Sound boring? I thought that way too before I tried it. At least give it a try.

—Katherine N., Suffolk Community College, New York

Set more than one alarm. If you don't know already, you're going to learn how to turn your alarm off in your sleep. I'm up to about eight alarms, and I finally wake up to the sixth one.

—Katherine N., Suffolk County Community College, New York

Don't be afraid to get to know your professors, especially if you're in a big lecture. Visit them during office hours and get yourself known—they have a lot of knowledge to share and are usually worth getting to know.

—Kerri C., SUNY Geneseo, New York

Promise yourself you'll find at least one new sport/activity to try. Meeting new people is hard, but getting involved can bring you closer to new friends and help you discover new interests. There's a world of possibilities on a college campus; all you have to do is find the courage to put yourself out there and try something new.

—Kerri C., SUNY Geneseo, New York

*If you can stay in a suite, **do it**. I am currently rooming with two other high school alumni in a freshman four-bedroom suite. Overall, I love living in my suite; it is 1,000 times better than any regular residency.*

—Ryan S., Florida Institute of Technology, Florida

*Go in with an open mind. In high school I was a very reserved kid and shy. I am currently a week or two away from being initiated into a fraternity. I had the stereotypical view that fraternity brothers are just party animals and tools, but this is **not** true. Deciding to pledge was the best decision I've made at college. I've made numerous friends, learned time management, learned how to deal with stress, and learned how to be a gentleman. Some advice would be to go to all the fraternities' rush events, and see if you like it. Some schools have hazing issues with fraternities, but at my school it has never been an issue. Fraternities are a great way to make friends, share values, enjoy school, and get involved.*

—Ryan S., Florida Institute of Technology, Florida

*It is important to get involved at school, but make sure that you join clubs that actually interest you. If you think that joining student government or becoming a member of the dance team is going to give you the best college experience, then you should do it because you want to, and not sit on the sidelines because somebody told you that was a bad idea. Make the most of your college experience in a way that **you** want to!*

—Courtney F., Hofstra University, New York

Get involved! I joined a lot of clubs when I got to school and made a lot of friends through them. Ski and outdoors club was great; I got to go skydiving and paintballing for an extremely discounted price. Student senate! It's not like high school senate; it's definitely a few steps up. You learn so much about the school nobody knows, and it's really interesting. Always try to move up in the organization, too; run for leadership positions! Play intramural sports—they're fun, laidback, and you meet a lot of people.

—**Steve C., York College of Pennsylvania**

Don't get distracted in your dorm room. I always used to keep my door open and talk to everyone on the floor instead of doing work and studying. So either close your door or go to the library. I never used the library in high school, but it was nice to utilize it in college and get work done.

—**Steve C., York College of Pennsylvania**

If you don't have a good time at orientation, it doesn't mean that you won't like the school. At orientation you don't meet even close to all the people that you will be interacting with on a daily basis when you start classes. Also, when school starts in the fall, you will have much more freedom than you did during orientation. So I think that it's important for people not to mistake bad experiences at orientation with the school and thinking that they will have a miserable time at school.

—**Courtney F., Hofstra University, New York**

I go to FitRec, BU's immaculate gym, three to four times per week.

—**Mike H., Boston University, Massachusetts**

My professor was there for me in my time of need; he talked to me for about an hour and then went on to tell me that the test could wait. I went home, and when I returned next semester, I took the exam. This event shaped my college experience so much! To see this side of a man I have only seen in a lecture of 300+ students amazed me.

—**Mike H., Boston University, Massachusetts**

Do not be discouraged if you don't get that 4.0 GPA—first semester is a period of adjustment, whether it's adjusting to a new town, new friends, or new living conditions. Once you get settled in and learn the ropes, classes will be a lot less nerve-wracking.

—**Kerri C., SUNY Geneseo, New York**

Reference Sheet H

About the college essay:

- *Try to stay within the requirements, i.e. 500 words.*
- *Try to be different. Stay away from the common topics, such as your football experience, a grandparent passing, why Catcher in the Rye is about you, etc.*
- *Sad topics are okay, but make sure to keep descriptions short.*
- *Always make sure to have the correct college name in your essay.*
- *The goal is to keep the reader interested, but try to keep away from topics that revolve around sex, drugs, and alcohol.*
- *You shouldn't start an essay with, "I know you want to have sex," etc. (FYI, it has happened before!)*
- *Remember that your essay is going to be read by other people at the college; therefore, you should make sure you're trying to impress the reader with your writing ability/potential and style.*
- *In most cases, the essay will be reviewed by the counseling office, first-year experience advisor, academic advisor, alumni giving department, and so on.*

Do's:

- *Speak in the first person. This is you talking. When referring to yourself, use the "I" pronoun; avoid using "you."*
- *Allow enough time to re-read the essay many times.*
- *Edit. Write and rewrite the essay to ensure clarity.*
- *Avoid details that confuse or add nothing.*
- *Read your essay aloud to hear how it sounds. Does it flow? Make sure it's your voice.*
- *Ask others to read your essay and give their feedback. Ask that feedback be constructive, such as, "I would love an example of that," "What happened next?", "This part confused me."*
- *Ask the reader how he felt after reading the entire college essay. His attitude will most likely be the same as that of the reader in the admissions office.*
- *Revise the ending to elicit the response you desire.*
- *With help, fix misspellings, errors, and unclear writing.*
- *Ensure that your style and personality are represented but don't allow errors.*

Dont's:

- *Do not exceed the word limit. Consider the reader. How would you feel if someone gave you more work to do?*
- *Avoid clichés. They don't distinguish you from other applicants, since a cliché is someone else's words.*
- *Avoid trying to say too much. Stick to one topic. Remember that you have an accomplishment list elsewhere in the application.*
- *Avoid a surfeit of "big" words.*
- *The topic of the college-admissions essay should be about you. While the college-application essay should be written to impress, it should avoid showing you in a pretentious light.*
- *Avoid slang.*
- *Remember, you're introducing yourself, not selling yourself.*

—Emmanuel Cruz, Admissions Counselor, Hartwick College, New York

I'm worried that I'm running out of time to get things done. Aside from school work, I have a part-time job, and I'm on two cheerleading teams. It is tough to balance my time, which I think hurts me because I've found myself rushing for deadlines and doing things last minute. I'm still very stressed because I still have things to do and I want to apply to more schools. I feel like I'm running out of time, and I feel like I'm annoying my guidance counselor by going to her office all of the time, which is kind of what holds me back from finishing my application process. I am very organized, I have kept myself organized throughout this whole process, and I know everything I still need to do, yet the only thing that still worries me is not finishing soon enough and colleges rejecting me because they didn't receive all of my materials.

—Victoria C., high school senior

Appendix C
Timeline

8th Grade

Reviewed/ Considered/ Completed	Recommendations	Time Frame
	Create a vigorous/strong course schedule for freshman year. Include honors and accelerated classes when possible.	Spring

9th Grade

Reviewed/ Considered/ Completed	Recommendations	Time Frame
	Participate in extracurricular activities. Keep a record/log of names, dates, statistics, and events.	All year
	Participate in leadership activities. Keep a record/log of names, dates, statistics, and hours.	All year
	Volunteer for community-service activities and events. Keep a record/log.	All year
	Reflect on personal interests and goals.	All year
	Maintain a file for all achievements, awards, and honors received.	All year
	Identify areas of interest and available elective courses.	Spring
	Create a vigorous/strong course schedule for sophomore year. Include honors and accelerated classes when possible.	Spring
	Earn highest course grades, which are reported on your official transcript.	All year

10th Grade

Reviewed/ Considered/ Completed	Recommendations	Time Frame
	Participate in extracurricular activities. Keep a record/log of names, dates, statistics, and events.	All year
	Volunteer for community-service activities and events. Keep a record/log of names, dates, statistics, and hours.	All year
	Participate in leadership activities. Keep a record/log of names, dates, statistics, and hours.	All year
	Reflect on personal interests and goals.	All year
	Contact college coaches with letters of interest.	All year
	Maintain a file for all achievements, awards, and honors received.	All year
	Earn highest course grades, which are reported on your official transcript.	All year
	Take the Preliminary SAT (PSAT).	Spring/when offered
	Identify areas of interest and available elective courses.	Spring
	Create a strong course schedule for junior year. Include honors, AP, IB, and college-level classes when possible.	Spring
	Participate in summer sports tournaments.	Summer
	Work part-time if your schedule allows.	After school/ weekends/ summer

11th Grade

Reviewed/ Considered/ Completed	Recommendations	Time Frame
	Take the Preliminary SAT (PSAT).	Fall/when offered
	Participate in extracurricular activities. Keep a record/log of names, dates, statistics, and events.	All year
	Participate in leadership activities. Keep a record/log of names, dates, statistics, and hours.	All year
	Volunteer for community-service activities and events. Keep a record/log of names, dates, statistics, and hours.	All year
	Reflect on personal interests and goals.	All year
	Attend college information sessions.	All year
	Attend recruitment events and tournaments.	All year
	Maintain contact with college coaches.	All year
	Maintain a file for all achievements, awards, and honors received.	All year
	Earn highest course grades, which are reported on your official transcript.	All year
	Complete scholarship applications.	All year
	Complete career interest and aptitude tests.	Spring
	Prepare for SAT/ACT exams.	4–6 weeks prior to exam date
	Register for and take College Admissions Tests, SAT/ACT.	Spring
	Register and take SAT subject tests.	Spring
	Request letters of recommendation.	Spring
	Attend college fairs.	Spring
	Attend pre-college planning meeting with guidance counselor and parents.	Spring
	Identify areas of interest and available elective courses.	Spring

	Create a strong course schedule for senior year. Include honors, AP, IB, and college-level classes when possible.	Spring
	Write your college essay.	Spring/summer
	Visit colleges if the opportunity is available.	Spring/summer
	Conduct preliminary research on colleges, financial aid, and scholarships.	Spring/summer
	Identify and apply for potential scholarship opportunities.	Spring/summer
	Participate in summer sports tournaments.	Summer
	Work part-time if your schedule allows.	After school/weekends/summer

12th Grade

Reviewed/ Considered/ Completed	Recommendations	Time Frame
	Worksheet 1: Student Questionnaire.	September
	Worksheet 2: Parent Questionnaire.	September
	Worksheet 3: Checklist for Students.	Fall
	Worksheet 4: Login/Password Organizer.	Fall
	Identify career interests and college majors.	September/October
	Worksheet 5: Checklist for Parents.	All year
	Register for college admissions tests, SAT/ACT.	September/October—watch deadlines
	Enroll in a SAT/ACT test-prep program/hire tutor.	4–6 weeks prior to exam date
	Understand college degrees, credits, and vocabulary.	September
	Attend college-application workshop, if offered.	Early fall
	Worksheet 6: School Services Questionnaire.	September

	Identify potential colleges.	September
	Attend college information sessions.	Fall
	Worksheet 19: College Visit Questionnaire.	When applicable
	Request letters of recommendation.	September
	Worksheet 10: Draft Request for Letter of Recommendation.	September
	Prepare for SAT/ACT exams.	4–6 weeks prior to exam date
	Worksheet 7: Putting It All Together.	September
	Meet with guidance counselor.	September
	Worksheet 8: Initial List of Schools.	September
	Begin online college applications.	September
	Take college admissions exams, SAT/ACT.	October, November, December
	Worksheet 9: Draft Activity Sheet.	October
	Worksheet 11: Categorizing Schools: Safety, Target, Reach, Shot in the Dark	October
	Self-report grades, if required.	November
	Attend college fairs.	Fall
	Write college-specific and short-response essays.	October
	Write/finalize college essay.	October
	Attend onsite registration/immediate-decision days.	When scheduled
	Attend on-campus college open houses.	Fall
	Worksheet 13: Your In-Progress Tracking Sheet.	October/November
	Attend state university college fair.	Fall
	Work part-time, if schedule allows.	After school/ weekends/summer

	Request official transcripts.	Fall
	Worksheet 14: Contact Info for Admission Offices.	Fall
	Analyze colleges' total cost of attendance.	Fall
	Worksheet 15: Personalized Total Cost of Attendance.	Fall
	Contact admissions office staff.	Fall/ongoing
	Finalize list of colleges.	October
	Identify local scholarship opportunities.	Fall
	Visit colleges you're considering.	Fall/winter
	Prepare activity sheet/resume.	October
	Request official test scores for SAT/ACT.	By application deadline
	Complete college applications and supplemental materials.	Early December
	Proofread your essay, application, and supplemental materials.	Constantly
	Complete CSS/financial-aid profile.	By application deadline
	Upload documents to application portal.	Fall
	Submit official applications. Pay fee.	By deadline
	Meet/communicate with guidance counselor.	All year
	Worksheet 16: Data Needed to Complete Net Price Calculator.	Fall
	Contact admissions office staff to express interest and address questions.	Fall
	Attend Financial Aid Night presentation.	Late fall
	Obtain your PIN for FAFSA.	December
	Identify and apply for scholarship opportunities.	All year

	Complete Free Application for Federal Student Aid (FAFSA).	January/February
	Maintain high grades/no senioritis!	Spring
	Compare financial-aid award packages.	Spring
	Worksheet 21: Rank Them: Pro or Con.	Spring
	Worksheet 20: Financial-Aid Award Comparison.	Spring
	Contact financial aid office staff for additional opportunities.	Spring
	Worksheet 22: Estimated Total Loans and Monthly Payments.	Spring
	Complete final scholarship applications.	By stated deadline
	Report all admission decisions to guidance counselor.	Spring
	Visit colleges where you've been accepted.	Spring
	Address college issues/awareness.	Spring/summer
	Make final decision and submit deposit.	By May 1st deadline
	Purchase college T-shirt/sweatshirt.	After final decision
	Remit on-campus housing forms and deposit.	As soon as possible
	Inform other schools that you will not be attending.	After final decision
	Meet graduation requirements.	June
	Schedule and attend orientation program/session.	Spring/summer
	Shop for college supplies.	Summer
	Work part-time, if schedule allows.	After school/weekends/summer

The whole process of completing college applications was very easy for me. I managed my time well and completed each part of my applications as early as I could. I realized the less you procrastinate, the better. My parents really only helped me pay for my applications; I filled them all out on my own.

—Brendan I., high school senior

At the end of last year, my parents and I were called down to guidance to start talking about my college application process. During this meeting I learned a lot about what needs to happen during this process and to start some things over the summer. I started to get a lot of community service done to make me look better for September when I start doing applications in the fall. When school started in September, I knew it was time to really start the process of applying to schools. My teacher, Ms. Portnoy, really made us get down to business and start looking at colleges and even filling out applications. I felt as though I needed more time, so I started my applications, but I wasn't sure of all the colleges I was applying to until the beginning of November. During the end of November, I finished all of my applications so that they would be in by December 1. I used the Common Application, and I felt it kept me focused because it let me fill out one application for all of my schools.

—Mark D., high school senior

INDEX